Tales from an Average Girl
The Messy Chronicles

Kimber Rose and Marie Devonn

Contents

Foreword

Please be advised that this book contains naughty language, intimate encounters (which might either tantalize or leave you wanting more—we appreciate your spirited enthusiasm and will strive to meet your desires), a cast of characters that includes both those we adore and those we can't help but despise, sprinklings of humor, dashes of sarcasm, poignant moments of sorrow, and regrettably, raw portrayals of real-life issues, including instances of abuse.

With this forewarning in hand, we invite you to immerse yourself in the world of an average girl in a very messy world.

The Postman Should Never Ring Twice

Nicole

Chapter One

Growing up, cousins often formed our earliest friendships, but my entry into this familial rite of passage was belated. All my cousins were significantly older, leaving me behind in shared experiences. It wasn't until I was 23 that I formed an unbreakable bond with one of my cousins, Nicole. Our connection blossomed unexpectedly, and soon, we were inseparable partners in crime in the truest sense.

Nicole, nine years my senior, had a distinct and captivating appearance. Her fair skin was the perfect canvas to highlight her striking hazel eyes, which sparkled with a blend of green and brown hues. For as long as I could remember, glasses had been a part of her signature look, each pair reflecting a facet of her dynamic personality. They weren't just an accessory but an extension of her tenacious spirit.

Standing at 5'6", she carried a sense of presence that belied her height, her curvy figure accentuating her confidence. Nicole treated her hair like a form of self-expression, always styled in a shoulder-length bob, but she loved experimenting with various colors and styles, each new look mirroring her mood or the latest chapter in her life.

Nicole, with her flamboyant and unapologetic approach to life, was always a character. In all truth, Nicole was a bit of a hoe. Now, before you go judging me, hear me out. She had a way of diving headfirst into the world of dating, often guided more by material desires than emotional connection. Her approach to relationships often focused on what a man could provide materially rather than what could be shared emotionally. It's fair to say that her choices in men often left much to be desired.

Among the multitude of suitors that paraded through her life, one stood out, in the worst way possible. His name is Ethan, however, in our circle, he is known as 'Postal Dude', or PD for short. While lacking in creativity, the nickname stuck and seemed fitting for the man who left such a memorable impression for all the wrong reasons.

Nicole's path crossed with PD in 2015, a fortuitous meeting that took place amid the mail-filled corridors of the postal service. It's here that the nickname 'Postal Dude' found its roots, an apt moniker for the man who would become a significant chapter in her life. From the outset, they were a perfect match, sharing common interests and an undeniable chemistry. I remember feeling a surge of hope for her; PD appeared to be a step up from her usual string of fleeting romances.

Their relationship escalated quickly. Who am I kidding?! They started dating, and by dating, I mean sleeping together. Despite my gentle prodding for Nicole to take things slow and get to know him, she was all in from the first date. The morning after, I was privy to every detail, her excitement painting a picture of a woman utterly captivated. I sometimes question if her heart lived in her vagina. Given Nicole's history, I harbored doubts about the longevity of this whirlwind romance, but as time passed, their connection seemed to deepen into something more substantial.

However, a year into their relationship, the initial enthusiasm had settled into a plateau of uncertainty. Nicole began to confide in me about her longing for a more profound commitment, her dreams of settling down, and even starting a family. I could sense her desire for a stable future, a significant departure from her usual carefree romances.

But there was a hitch in her plan. Despite the intimacy they shared, Nicole's presence in PD's life seemed confined to the weekends. Her belongings, like herself, were temporary fixtures in his house, disappearing by the start of each week. PD was dragging his feet using the typical excuses of "Why should we mess up a good thing?" or "I want the same things you do, but I don't want to rush and screw things up between us as I have done in the past." This arrangement, to me, was a red flag waving high. A man who insists on keeping his living space devoid of any trace of his partner hints at secrets lurking beneath the surface.

Am I the only one seeing the red flags here, as clear as day?

Yet, Nicole, lost in the chaos of her feelings, was blind to the warning signs. It felt like watching a car hurtling towards an inevitable crash, and despite my desperate internal screams for it to stop, the disaster was unavoidable. I stood witness to this unfolding drama, my heart heavy with the suspicion of impending heartache.

Chapter Two

Nicole's attempts to steer their relationship towards a more committed future seemed to echo unheard in PD's ears with each passing week. That is, until one unexpected afternoon when she called me, bubbling with ecstatic joy. Her excitement was infectious, and we agreed to meet for dinner to celebrate and delve into the details.

I had barely exited my car at the restaurant when Nicole bounded towards me, her hand thrust forward to reveal a sparkling engagement ring. Looking at the ring, and seeing the unmistakable radiance of pure joy on Nicole's face, I felt foolish for ever doubting PD.

"So, spill the details!" I urged, my curiosity piqued.

Looking back, I was in no way prepared for the story I was about to hear, and neither are you.

She began her story as we sat at our table and ordered two Margaritas. "We went to Grand Lux Café on Saturday evening," she began, her eyes alight with the memory. "It is my absolute favorite place. It is like the Cheesecake Factory but grander. We were deep in conversation about our future, something I never thought he'd be open to, and then..." Her voice trembled with emotion. "After dessert, I returned from the restroom to find a little black box beside my plate. It was like a scene from a romantic movie – he was on one knee, the ring gleaming, the whole restaurant bursting into applause when I said 'yes.'"

My heart swelled for her happiness, though a part of me couldn't shake the feeling that it was all too surreal, like a page out of a fairy tale. But everyone deserves their fairy-tale moment, right?! As Nicole continued, detailing every aspect of her engagement, I couldn't help but notice the ring. It was elegant yet understated – a gold band with a pear-shaped diamond – not quite Nicole's usual flamboyant style. Nicole has always been one of those women where everything she owned had to have a label.

Curious, I asked to take a closer look at the ring. As she slipped the ring off, an interesting engraving caught my eye, "All We Need C & L 04/10/95." The mysterious initials sent my mind reeling. Who the hell were C and L? The question hung in the air, unspoken yet heavily present, adding an unexpected twist to what was already an unbelievable tale.

As I held the ring, puzzling over the engraving, it struck me – the initials "C & L" were a mystery, unrelated to Nicole or Ethan. My confusion was evident, and noticing my perplexed expression, Nicole pressed, "What's wrong?"

"Nicole, who the fuck are C & L?" I blurted out, unable to mask my surprise. She flushed a deep red and quickly reclaimed the ring, muttering, "I should never have let you see it."

"What does that mean?" I pressed, my curiosity turning to concern. Nicole hesitated, clearly torn between honesty and holding back.

"Nicole, you can trust me. What's the story with this ring?" I urged gently.

With a heavy sigh and a swig of her margarita, she recounted her past few blissful weeks with PD; a tale that left me questioning every aspect of their relationship. According to Nicole, postal workers like her and PD often team up for longer routes. It had become routine for her and PD to work a route together. This is the first I have heard of this, but it is a common occurrence for them. During one such shift, Nicole found a ring in the grass near a mailbox. While any normal person, myself included, would have sought its rightful owner, PD had other plans – he kept the ring, intending to assess its value for potential sale.

I was screaming internally at this point. The sheer audacity of their plan was shocking. "Who the fuck does that?" I thought, appalled at the idea of not returning the ring to its owner.

Nicole revealed that PD had held onto the ring for five months.

Yes, I said that correctly. FIVE MONTHS! Now, let's do that math! She discovered the ring around month 11 of their relationship, as they were 16 months in at this point. He had a whole five months to make a decision about the ring – whether to return it or even stick to the initial plan of selling it to purchase a ring for my cousin. The possibilities were wide open for an ass like him.

I fumed as the unfortunate truth continued to hit me like a ton of bricks – PD had proposed to Nicole with a ring she found, a ring that belonged to someone else. What an absolute asshole!

"Nicole, do you realize how insane this sounds?" I asked, incredulous. "How can you accept a ring that's not even meant for you, one that he didn't bother to buy himself? Hell, he could have gone to Walmart. He could've chosen any ring that genuinely symbolized his commitment to you. This is absolute bullshit!"

I could see my words struck a chord as tears welled in her eyes. Her voice trembled with a mix of defiance and heartbreak, "Why can't you just be happy for me?"

"Because this doesn't sit right with me," I replied, my voice clear with concern. "You deserve so much better than this. I don't understand why you can't see that."

Her response was silent but profound – she gathered her belongings and left the restaurant without another word. I remained there, stunned, grappling with the magnitude of what I had just learned. It marked the beginning of a seven-month silence between us, a painful gap in a relationship once so close.

Chapter Three

Despite my earnest attempts, Nicole remained unreachable, ignoring my calls and messages. I wrestled with a sense of guilt over my blunt words, yet a part of me felt no regret. Someone needed to speak up, and I've never been one to shy away from the truth. In my eyes, PD was nothing but trouble, a conclusion hard to ignore. Deep down, I wondered if it was my place to intervene. Honestly, could anyone stand by silently in such a situation?

I had almost resigned myself to the possibility that Nicole might never reconnect with me, especially while she was with PD It was a tough pill to swallow, missing the bond we once shared. But in my heart, I understood her silence, painful as it was. Letting go, I realized, is sometimes the only way to let someone you love find their path.

Imagine my shock when a familiar ring of the doorbell shattered the quiet of a Saturday evening seven months later. Standing there was Nicole, her eyes brimming with tears, surrounded by her bags.

"Nicole," I called out softly, beckoning her inside. She stepped in, and we embraced, her sobs filling the room as I held her close. Once she calmed down, I helped her with her bags and led her to the living room. Settling on the couch, I gently prodded, "Nicole, what happened? Tell me everything." Through her tears, I glimpsed the noticeable absence of her engagement ring. "What happened with Ethan?" I pressed, handing her a box of tissues.

Dabbing her eyes, and blowing her nose, Nicole began to tell me the circumstances that had led her here. Two weeks after our ill-fated dinner, she had moved in with PD. Their life seemed to be aligning; they shared morning commutes to the post office, their conversations filled with plans for a small destination wedding in Jamaica, and they even started redecorating his house to make it feel more like a home for both of them. It all appeared to be the steps of a couple profoundly planning a future together.

Three months into their cohabitation, Nicole began to notice unsettling shifts in PD's behavior, the classic signs that trouble was brewing. As women, we have an innate sense of when our significant other is up to no good. His phone became an object of secrecy; calls were taken in hushed tones in another room, late nights at work became frequent, and errands seemed to pop up out of nowhere—all classic signs of infidelity.

Given their shared commutes, Nicole was puzzled by how PD managed these late hours. But then, around the fifth month of living together, he claimed that a sudden change in his work schedule prevented them from traveling together to work anymore. It all sounded too convenient, too calculated. As days turned into weeks, Nicole's unease grew. Conversations about wedding plans, once filled with excitement and anticipation, dwindled to nothing. PD would skillfully dodge the conversation whenever she broached the topic or found an excuse to leave the room.

The tipping point came two weeks ago when Nicole's engagement ring vanished. After returning from work, she removed the ring for a shower and, exhausted, forgot to put it back on. The following day, the ring was nowhere to be found on the bathroom counter. PD had already left for work, so she texted him, only to receive a dismissive reply that it must be somewhere in the house. His abrupt end to the conversation when she pressed further only deepened her suspicion.

The confrontation between Nicole and PD later that day erupted into a fiery clash. PD, with a cunning twist of words, deflected the blame onto Nicole. He accused her of negligence and a lack of appreciation, weaving his words in a way that left her apologizing, a victim of his manipulative tactics. The ring, once a symbol of their commitment, now stood as a testament to her alleged carelessness in his eyes, a stark reminder of PD's startling absence of empathy.

Resigned and disheartened, Nicole accepted the loss of the ring as an unfortunate reality. Yet, when she tentatively mentioned replacing the ring, PD's response was cold and cutting. "Why would I buy you another ring when you couldn't even take care of the first one?" he scoffed. This callous retort, dismissive and cruel, was a piercing blow to her already fragile emotions.

I was dumbfounded. I literally felt like I needed to pick my jaw up off the floor. My first thought upon hearing this was, "It wasn't like you bought the first ring, you thief!" Then I began to question how Nicole, who had always been quick to stand up for herself, could tolerate such treatment. The Nicole I knew wouldn't have hesitated to walk away from less. Watching her succumb to PD's manipulation was both heartbreaking and infuriating.

"Nicole, tell me what happened today. What made you leave?" I gently prodded, noticing the glisten of tears cascading down her cheeks. She murmured in a voice barely louder than a whisper, laden with disbelief and sorrow, "I wasn't the only one."

Chapter Four

My expression must have mirrored my shock, but I held my tongue, allowing her to unfold the story at her own pace. She took a deep breath and began, "Today was supposed to be about our future, about picking out gifts for our wedding. But then, out of the blue, he said he had to work. I thought nothing of it, so I decided to postpone the registry. He was in a hurry, almost frantic, and in his rush, he left his phone behind."

She paused, collecting her thoughts. "I was browsing wedding dresses when his phone buzzed. The screen lit up with a name I didn't recognize – Sandra. Before I could react, the call ended, and texts began to appear, their content teasingly hidden. Phrases about meeting a caterer and lunch plans floated up, each word a dagger to my heart."

Nicole's voice quivered as she recounted Ethan's return. "I was snapped back to reality by the sound of the front door opening. He was flustered as he dashed into the room. He grabbed his phone, saying he'd forgotten it," she continued. "I was seething inside, a storm of emotions raging, but I played it cool, asking if he had everything he needed this time. He hurriedly assured me he did and left again.

The urge to confront him was overpowering, but Nicole knew she needed evidence. Grabbing her keys, she followed him stealthily, a silent observer of the unfolding truth. Her heart pounded as she trailed his car to Cyclone Anaya's. There, the final blow was dealt – Ethan with another woman, their embrace intimate, undeniable.

Fueled by a blend of fury and heartache, Nicole confronted them. "Ethan, what the hell is this?" she demanded, her voice a tone of pure rage. Their faces registered shock, but the sight of her engagement ring adorning the other woman's finger sent Nicole over the edge. In that instant, the depth of Ethan's betrayal was laid bare, the cruel reality of his deceit exposed in broad daylight.

The world around Nicole blurred as the crushing weight of truth settled in. The ring, a symbol of their supposed love, was now a token of his infidelity – a revelation that shattered her world into a million pieces.

Nicole's eyes meticulously scanned the woman from head to toe. Their builds had an unquestionable resemblance – both medium height and blessed with curves in all the right places. The woman's darker complexion was beautifully offset by her long curly hair, highlighted to perfection, complementing her deep brown eyes. Despite the tension, Nicole couldn't help but acknowledge her striking beauty.

A wave of raw emotion brought Nicole back from her dazed observation. Fueled by an intense, blind fury, she demanded, "Is this Sandra?" Her voice was sharp, cutting through the air like a knife.

The woman, emanating a mixture of defiance and confidence, stepped forward. "Who's asking?" she challenged, her posture unyielding as she stepped around PD to confront Nicole head-on.

"I'm his fiancée!" Nicole declared, her words tinged with a venomous edge.

The woman let out a mocking laugh. "You've got jokes. I'm his fiancée. You're clearly delusional. This man is mine, and I suggest you go back to wherever you crawled out from," she sneered.

The absurdity of the situation intensified as Nicole, her anger reaching a boiling point, retorted, "I have been with this man for almost two years! We've been planning our wedding, and that ring you're wearing? It's mine. He didn't even buy it – I found it on a postal route!"

The woman's face twisted into a look of cold disdain. "Believe whatever fantasy you want, but that's just ridiculous. What kind of woman even accepts a ring found on the street? You're clearly lying."

I thought, "Who lies about something as embarrassing as that?"

Nicole shot back sharply, "I don't know, why you don't believe me? 'your' ring was lying there in the dirt. Did you even bother to read the inscription inside the band?"

The woman responded defensively, "First of all, it's none of your concern. But for your information, this ring belonged to Ethan's mother, given to her for her vow renewal. That explains the inscription."

Nicole glanced over at PD, whose expression silently conveyed a triumphant 'Checkmate.'

I listened, my mind reeling upon hearing the unbelievable scene my cousin described. I was dumbfounded by the audacity and foolishness of it all. How dumb could both of them be?! My cousin, usually so composed, detailed a confrontation that seemed straight out of a dramatic screenplay. Part of me ached for Nicole, while another part had sensed the inevitable implosion of her relationship with PD and I had tried to warn her, but my attempts fell on deaf ears.

The verbal altercation quickly escalated, their voices rising, attracting a crowd outside the restaurant. Driven by fury and desperation, Nicole, hell-bent on reclaiming her ring, lunged at the woman with extreme determination. As they wrestled, the scene descended into chaos, with onlookers gasping and murmuring.

As I heard the dramatic retelling, I sat bewildered, unable to fathom why they were viciously battling over a ring that, in truth, belonged to neither of them.

In the heat of their struggle, Nicole's gaze once again caught PD standing aside, his smirk betraying a sense of twisted satisfaction. It was a chilling sight – him deriving pleasure from the spectacle he had orchestrated.

The realization hit Nicole like a tidal wave. She abruptly stopped fighting, her body tensing as she locked eyes with PD "You sick bastard! You are actually enjoying this!?" she accused, her voice a mix of horror and disgust.

As I listened intently, struggling desperately to control my facial expressions, I was astounded at the sheer audacity and how twisted PD was. He had manipulated not one but two

PD, seeing his ploy unraveling, quickly shifted gears, embracing the other woman protectively. "Babe, she's insane! Remember the coworker I told you about and why I had to change my work schedule? The one obsessed with me? That's her. She's completely delusional," he lied smoothly, pulling the woman closer.

Nicole's face, a canvas of shock and realization, reflected the depth of betrayal she felt. The other woman, clinging to PD, added insult to injury. "I knew she was crazy! She's lucky I don't call the cops on her. We should've dealt with her long ago," she spat out maliciously.

In that moment of painful clarity, Nicole recognized the two years with PD for what they were – a beautifully woven tapestry of lies. Drained and defeated, she delivered her parting words with a heavy heart. "You two are made for each other. But mark my words; one day, you'll find yourself in my shoes, facing the same deceit." With those final words, she turned and walked away, leaving their mocking jeers behind.

Nicole told me she cried uncontrollably during the entire drive, tears blurring the road ahead. She drove without direction until she almost instinctively found herself at my doorstep, seeking refuge in the only place she felt safe.

***

In the wake of the explosive events, I set up a sanctuary for Nicole in my guest room, offering her a haven as she navigated through her storm of emotions. The weeks that followed were a quiet period of healing and reflection. Nicole, seeking to distance herself from the painful memories tied to PD, requested a transfer to another post office. Fortune smiled upon her plight, granting her request within a mere three weeks.

Those interim weeks, however, were far from easy. Working in close proximity to PD was a constant torment for Nicole. His presence was a relentless reminder of the betrayal and pain she had endured. He made several attempts to reach out, claiming his love for the other woman was non-existent and that his actions were born of panic. But each encounter, each word he uttered, only served to reopen the wounds Nicole was desperately trying to heal.

Nicole moved through those days like a ghost, her spirit dimmed by the shadows of her recent past. On her days off, she confined herself to her room, emerging only for brief moments to eat before retreating back into her self-imposed isolation. Watching her, I felt a growing concern for her well-being. The approval of her transfer couldn't have come at a more crucial time.

The change in her work environment gradually began to dispel the fog of despair that had enveloped Nicole. Slowly but surely, the light returned to her eyes, and the semblance of the vibrant woman I knew started to re-emerge. Each day at her new post brought a little more of her back to life.

Nicole had found an apartment close to work by the third month in her new role. She began to reacquaint herself with the world outside, tentatively at first, but with growing confidence. Her social calendar started to fill, and I found myself being whisked away to various events around town. While the frequent outings were a bit much for me, seeing her smile and laugh again was a joy. Nicole was reclaiming her life, and it was a beautiful sight.

Life isn't perfect, and the notion of "happily ever after" often exists only in the pages of storybooks. The complex nature of reality has a way of weaving unexpected turns, and Nicole's journey was a testament to this truth. However, her past, a landscape filled with unresolved chapters and lingering shadows, was not yet ready to release its hold on her just yet...

Am I His Brother's Keeper?

Kim

Chapter Five

It had been ages since I last connected with Kim. She had weathered a stormy marriage riddled with infidelity, culminating in a tumultuous divorce. I never held her husband in high regard, feeling deep down that she was worthy of so much more. His departure, frankly, was a relief to me. However, the chaos and pain he left behind were far from welcome. Throughout her ordeal, I stood by Kim, offering support and solace. Today we were meeting for our long-overdue girls' night – a monthly tradition recently put on hold due to her circumstances.

Settling into our dinner, Kim and I quickly fell into our familiar rhythm of laughter and storytelling, catching up on the myriad of moments we had missed in each other's lives. However, amidst our light-hearted banter, the conversation inevitably veered towards Kim's recent divorce. I noticed a hesitation in her, a pause that hinted at unspoken truths. Leaning in, I gently probed, "Kim, with all that's happened, it might seem trivial to ask, but are you truly okay?"

It was as though my question had touched a hidden trigger within her. Kim looked at me with a deep, resigned sigh and said, "You don't know the full story." I leaned back, my eyes widening in anticipation as Kim began filling in the gaps of what I had only assumed to be the complete narrative of her marriage's undoing.

Kim had never imagined herself capable of such a profound betrayal, of crossing a line she once deemed sacred. Yet, life's unpredictable twists had led her down an unthinkable path – she found herself in a secret affair with her husband's brother. The origins of this forbidden romance were murky, even to her; it had all started so innocuously.

What began with simple in-law interactions punctuated by flirtatious exchanges evolved into a private world of shared cheeky memes and covert meetings. Before long, Kim found herself irresistibly drawn to her brother-in-law's magnetic charm, a powerful and unexpected pull that left her reeling. Their connection, forbidden and fraught with complexity, deepened with each stolen moment.

The tipping point came on Thanksgiving, a day marked by family and gratitude, which ironically became the backdrop for the consummation of their secret relationship. It was a moment that changed everything, a point of no return in the tangled web of their illicit affair.

***

With her delicate frame and striking brunette locks, Kim carried an effortless grace that often drew admiring glances, just as her husband Sam fondly noted. Her eyes sparkled with life, her smile radiating warmth like the first light of dawn. Her approach to makeup was minimal, accentuating rather than altering her natural beauty.

That Thanksgiving, Kim chose a dress that seemed tailor-made for her - a low-cut, earthy brown number that embraced her figure like a second skin, echoing the goddess-like aura she felt within. As she entered the Anderson family home, arm in arm with Sam, she couldn't help but notice the subtle, appreciative glances from some of the men in the room. Her elegant stride and the gentle sway of her dress accentuated her shapely legs, drawing admiring looks.

Alexander, Sam's older brother, was a man who carried his athletic build with a certain poise. His features were sharply defined, a testament to his rugged handsomeness. His dark hair was kept short, adding to his tidy, composed appearance. The suit he wore that day was crafted just for him, perfectly emphasizing his broad shoulders and lean frame. There was an unmistakable vibrancy in his eyes, a reflection of a passionate soul.

As Kim crossed the room, she felt the weight of Alexander's gaze on her – a look so intense it was almost palpable. She sensed a hint of desire in his eyes, a spark of attraction that seemed to leap across the room. Later, in a moment of candid vulnerability, Alexander confessed to Amber that he saw her as the most beautiful woman he had ever encountered, expressing a yearning to be near her. Kim was acutely aware of his eyes following her every move, intensifying their unspoken connection.

Alexander himself felt spellbound by Kim's allure, drawn in by her captivating presence. The space around them seemed charged with a carnal energy, a mutual recognition of an attraction that defied convention.

As Kim and Alexander's eyes locked, an intense and undeniable chemistry surged between them. The atmosphere was thick with unexpressed need, each glance and subtle gesture amplifying the growing tension. Alexander felt a fiery rush of lust coursing through his veins as he admired Kim's irresistible allure. The raw, primal urge to be close to her, to feel her touch, consumed his thoughts, pushing aside the reality that she was his brother's wife. He craved her in a way that was both passionate and possessive.

Chapter Six

The house was alive with the bustle of Thanksgiving festivities. The sounds of movies and card games occupied the family. Alexander seized the moment and discreetly guided Kim upstairs, away from the prying eyes of the family. Equally fascinated by Alexander's hypnotic charm, Kim felt an enticing pull towards him. She lost herself in the thought of being with him. She wanted him to kiss her and make her forget the rest of the world. She wanted everything he could give her. She was ready for him.

Alone in the room, behind a locked door, the air was brimming with their sexual tension. Their proximity heightened every sensation, their breathing becoming more labored as they drew closer. Alexander gazed deeply into Kim's eyes, his own filled with an ardent longing. He pushed Amber against the wall facing away from him. Kim could feel Alexander's tongue run down the side of her neck as he stretched her dress to slide it down her body.

Kim felt a thrilling wave of anticipation wash over her. Her body quivered as Alexander's hands made their way back up to her full bottom and squeezed, his actions filled with an intense need. She could feel his fingers graze the wetness of her slit, amplifying the ache now growing between her legs.

He turned her around and ran his fingers across her lips so Kim could taste the sweetness of her juices. Kim's tongue instinctively brushed across them, savoring the taste in her mouth. He bit his lip as he watched her, imagining what more her tongue could do. The thought of Kim's mouth wrapped around his cock sent a rush of blood to his already engorged erection.

The intensity of their connection was overwhelming. Alexander couldn't help but kiss her. It nearly took her breath away. Lost in the moment, their kisses deepened, passionate and all-consuming, as their caresses grew more explorative, more intimate. Moving away from Kim's mouth, Alexander, eager to explore her body, began kissing her neck, playfully biting and sucking.

Kim, unable to stand the teasing of Alexander's mouth, began pulling at his clothes. She ripped his shirt open to reveal his chiseled pecks and abs. Her hands ran across his bare chest, completely enraptured by the feel of every contour. In this moment, he seemed perfect, and an overwhelming, almost urgent craving that demanded fulfillment washed over her.

Alexander watched as Kim marveled at his body. As her hands made their way down his body, across his abs and to his belt, she was almost salivating at the thought of freeing the growing bulge straining against the inside of his pants. Alexander grabbed her hands, pinning them over her head. His gaze held a devilish yet fierce flame as he kissed her deeply.

"Do you want me to fuck you?" Alexander said between kisses.

Without hesitation, Kim replied, "Yes." Alexander embodied her ideal, and at that point, her only want was to surrender to him entirely, to satisfy the longing that had taken hold of her.

"Yes, what, slut?" Alexander said, biting Amber's lip.

He had an insatiable need to claim her, to make her his in every sense. "Yes, Daddy," Kim said, sending a shiver of anticipation through her. He could sense her excitement building, her body trembling slightly, caught up in the moment and eagerly awaiting the intimacy to unfold. Kim knew this was it as she bent her head against the wall, her eyes closed as he kissed her neck.

Kim's beauty enraptured Alexander, his desire for her growing with each passing second. He spun her around, making her bend over with her legs apart and hands touching the floor. Kim could hear as Alexander undid his belt and his zipper sliding down. She saw his pants drop to the floor. She turned to look only to be met with a smack on each ass cheek. She moaned as a mix of pain and pleasure radiated through her, causing the growing wetness to spread down her thighs.

Alexander felt his desire increasing even more as she stood bent over before him. It was as if it was his destiny to take this woman and make her come until she couldn't anymore. He stroked his rigid member taking in the sight before him as he brushed his cock near the damp slit between Kim's legs. The more he teased Kim, brushing his cock back and forth, grazing her bud, the more she rocked her hips in hopes of sweet relief. Watching her do this made him want to punish her and draw the inevitable out forever.

However, the closeness of her vagina and the warmth emanating from it beckoning his member was intoxicating. As he positioned himself at her entrance, they knew there was no turning back from their chosen path.

He slid his hands down to her hips, and with one forceful thrust, he slid deep inside of Kim. He basked in the feeling of being inside of her. It was far beyond anything he ever expected. Kim was lost in the sensation of his impressive manhood molding her around him, making her perfect just for him. They were spellbound by this illicit moment, oblivious to everything else, focusing solely on the exhilarating feel of skin against skin as their bodies moved in perfect harmony.

For Kim, the experience was like a vivid dream, her body and mind awash with pleasure. She was his. He was entirely in control. He was going to make her his with each thrust. He could feel her melting into him.

Kim gasped, feeling an overwhelming intensity as Alexander moved within her with a depth and skill that seemed to touch her very soul. She surrendered herself to him, offering her body to him.

"I wanted him to take me; I needed him to take me. I wanted to experience all of him for myself. He was mine, if only for that moment," Kim said, reminiscing.

"I'm sorry... what?!"

Chapter Seven

The words barely escaped my lips, a whisper of astonishment after Kim's admission. My shock, however, seemed to dissolve into the air unnoticed. Amber, lost in vividly recalling that intimate, albeit forbidden memory, remained oblivious to my surprise.

Kim seemed almost entranced as she recounted when Alexander brought his body closer to hers. They were face to face, the warmth radiating from her skin discernible. As she exhaled, a hint of cinnamon lingered between them, tantalizing his senses. Her eyes, heavy with desire, were half-closed, and her breaths came in deep, rapid waves. Kim had surrendered entirely then, crossing a point of no return. Pressed against the wall, feeling the entirety of his cock enter her again, she was lost in the sensation and wished he could stay inside of her forever.

Alexander found himself completely immersed in her, unable to resist, unwilling to stop. Every sensation was magnified, every touch a revelation.

Kim's body trembled in anticipation, on the brink of a climax that now seemed inevitable, culminating in their shared passion. Alexander was acutely aware that through their union, she was approaching a peak of ecstasy. His hands explored her with urgency, his movements becoming more fervent, driven by their mutual desire.

Their bodies entwined in a dance of raw passion, adrift in a world of their own making, leaving only the intense need to satisfy their deep-seated longing. Their breaths were quick and shallow, hearts beating frantically as they surrendered to the overwhelming tide of desire.

Snapping back to the present, Kim's voice held a reflective tone, "At that moment, it was as if we stepped into a hidden, forbidden realm where only the two of us existed. We both knew there was a steep price for entering this secret world, but those concerns seemed trivial in the face of such an undeniable connection. We were prepared to face any consequence, pay whatever the price for that profound bond we shared."

I sat there, wide-eyed, feeling like a deer caught in headlights. "How could you keep this from me?" I asked, a tinge of hurt in my voice.

Kim sighed, a complex mix of emotions playing across her face. "At the time, it felt impossible to share. Each encounter left me with a sense of guilt, especially towards his innocent wife. You know how it was with Sam – he's was unfaithful since day one. Here we are, 25 years later, and he's still hot and heavy with most of the whores in our town. I'm not saying that makes my actions okay; two wrongs don't make a right. I just needed something for myself, something secret that he would never discover, but would wound him deeply if he did. I guess it was my way of getting back at him, a kind of revenge. I didn't want to change how you saw me, or have you judge me for my actions."

I couldn't help but empathize deeply with Kim as I reached across the table for her hand. She had spent her prime years with a man who neither deserved nor appreciated her worth. With a tinge of sadness and a hint of regret, Kim continued her story.

Our affair was like a dream, a secret world where passion and desire reigned supreme. I was living on the edge, addicted to the adrenaline of our secret encounters. The intensity of our encounters and our unquestionable chemistry were all overpowering. Even though I knew it was wrong, the temptation was too strong to resist, and I was caught in a never-ending storm of longing and desire.

Time seemed to fly as we continued our secret liaisons, each meeting more intense than the last. I tried to resist, but the affair took over my life, leading me down a dangerous path of unfaithfulness. My relationship with Alexander became more consuming even as I tried to end it. Eventually, the inevitable happened – my husband discovered that his brother was the other man in my life. Alexander implored me to stay with him on the fateful night we were discovered, claiming we were destined to be together. Then my husband walked in, and our lives took an irrevocable turn. That discovery shattered our marriages apart, leaving a wake of anger, betrayal, and profound sadness.

In the midst of my crumbling marriage, an unexpected bond formed with my sister-in-law, Elizabeth. Instead of resentment and bitterness, we found solace and strength within each other, united by the pain and disillusionment caused by our husbands. I spent countless hours expressing my remorse, trying to make her understand that my actions were never meant to cause her pain. With their charming façade and history of infidelity, the Anderson brothers had been a formidable force, but I naively underestimated the full impact of our intertwined lives.

Kim's revelations echoed in my mind as we settled into our meal. I had always assumed her marriage unraveled solely due to Sam's chronic infidelity. But now, understanding that her affair with his brother was the decisive blow to their already fragile union, the past events clicked into place, fitting together like pieces of a complex puzzle.

The sudden cancellations of our girls' nights, the mysterious pickups from unusual locations, and the carefully crafted cover stories for Sam – it all made sense now. I had always sensed Kim's unhappiness and suspected she might be seeing someone else. Yet, the confession that the 'someone else' was her husband's brother was beyond anything I could have imagined.

While I did not judge Kim's choices, I had mixed feelings about the situation. It was a lot to process, and my margarita seemed pathetically inadequate to handle the task.

In the wake of Kim's and Alexander's affair, a chaotic blend of emotions raged - a mix of regret, guilt, and the persistent question: What were they thinking? It was a time of deep self-reflection for Kim, questioning how her desires had completely overpowered her judgment. The divorce was a tumultuous blow, but in this period of upheaval, Kim found an unexpected ally in her sister-in-law. Their shared experiences with the Anderson brothers forged a bond that transcended traditional familial ties.

Kim reflected, "My affair with Alexander, driven by a vortex of anger, hurt, and a yearning for retribution, only complicated our emotional entanglement further. The Anderson brothers' notoriety for infidelity was no secret in our small town. Yet, there was an unspoken expectation for us to overlook it. We both suffered the same deceit and the harrowing journey of rebuilding ourselves. We became bonded by a mutual sense of betrayal, we discovered a connection that was more than physical; it was emotional, even spiritual. It was a bond that mended the wounds left by our broken relationships. Though divorcing our spouses was a path we never anticipated, it opened the door to a new chapter we could embark upon together, united and resilient. In each other's company, we found understanding and solace that transcended the pain of our past. Our friendship evolved into a healing love."

I couldn't help but smile, proud that Kim had emerged resilient from her chaotic journey. I also felt deeply grateful for the strong bond that had blossomed between her and her sister-in-law, enabling them to navigate the storm together. The familiar ring of Kim's phone suddenly interrupted my reflections on their ordeal.

"Hey," Kim answered, her voice brimming with excitement. "Yeah, we're in the back. See you soon."

As she ended the call, curiosity got the better of me. "Who was that?" I inquired.

A hint of nervousness flickered across Kim's face as she replied, "I know we're catching up, but there's someone I really wanted you to meet."

Intrigued, I couldn't help but tease a little. "Is this a 'friend' or a friend?" I asked, emphasizing the word 'friend' with air quotes.

Kim sidestepped my question, her plea simple, "Please be nice!"

I laughed, responding in jest, "Aren't I always?"

Just then, a strikingly handsome man in a business suit approached. He was an impressive figure, a stark contrast to Sam. I found myself approving instantly. Kim stood up with an infectious smile, but to my surprise, she greeted a woman who followed him. My confusion must have been evident as I waited for an introduction.

"Brooke," Kim began, pausing slightly, "This is Liz."

As I stood to embrace Liz, a thought nagged at me. "The sister-in-law?" I questioned, stepping back from our hug.

Kim and Liz exchanged a glance, a silent communication passing between them. Kim's voice was hesitant as she confirmed, "Yeah, my sister-in-law, well, ex-sister-in-law."

A brief, awkward silence fell over us. It was clear that there was more to this story, evident in how Kim and Liz looked at each other, their eyes locked in a hushed exchange.

Breaking the silence, Kim began again, her voice tinged with emotion, "Brooke..." She paused, gathering her thoughts. "Liz is my fiancée."

Trapped in the Closet

Paige

Chapter Eight

As the unofficial president of the Ride or Die Friendship Club, I take my duties very seriously—well, sort of. Picture this: I've got a superhero cape with mismatched socks and a sidekick who's just as likely to bail me out of jail as she is to join me in breaking into spontaneous dance-offs at the grocery store. Being a ride-or-die friend means I've perfected the art of enthusiastically saying, "Hold my purse and watch this!" just before executing questionable life decisions. So, if you need someone to help you bury a secret, hide from an ex, or embark on a quest for the perfect late-night snack, I'm your girl, armed with snacks, sarcasm, and an undying commitment to the chaos of true friendship.

It was a Saturday night like any other. I was lying in bed eating Oreos and watching The Golden Girls when my friend Paige texted me "911" to pick her up from the other side of town. It was just past 9 PM, and in typical Paige fashion, the shit had hit the fan. I grabbed my cape and mismatched socks without hesitation and hit the road. I made the 45-minute drive with no questions asked.

I found Paige standing outside a sketchy-looking apartment complex. But that's Paige for you; she thrives on adventures with bad boys. Paige began her tale of woe as she hopped into my car and fastened her seatbelt. I had barely pulled off before I heard, "Girl, this asshole put me in a damn closet, and I ended up pissing myself on the damn closet floor!" she declared, the gravity of her words masked by a playful eyeroll. My laughter bubbled up as I prodded her for the entire account, insisting she start from the beginning.

Paige rolled her eyes again, with a hint of playful exasperation, as we navigated out of the questionable apartment parking lot. "You know, today was one of the craziest and most messed-up days I've ever had in my entire life," she confessed. "It is ironic, considering the weekend started with such promise. We explored the town, shared laughter over dinners, and strolled along the city streets of Downtown Houston talking.

In dramatic Paige fashion, she starts, "Let me set the stage for how this crazy ass day started. I had just gotten out of the shower and wrapped myself in the towel Devin left for me. I made my way down the hallway to Devin's bedroom. I couldn't help but admire the sight of this delicious– caramel-colored man with perfectly toned arms and legs. He's not a gym rat, but clearly someone who takes care of himself, you know. He peacefully slept across the bed because you know your girl got that NyQuil to ensure a peaceful night's sleep," she teased.

At that, I burst into laughter and quipped, "Oh, really now?! Is it prescription strength?"

With a mix of frustration and humor, Paige shot back, "Can I please continue with the disaster that is my life?!"

With an amused smile and a theatrical wave of my hand, I replied, "By all means, do continue."

Paige starts again. "I grabbed the blunt we didn't finish earlier from the dresser and lit it, ensuring not to disturb him. I've been itching to explore his apartment since I arrived Friday because something seemed off, like a woman lived there, but hey, I gave him the benefit of the doubt.

"You mean you had already given him your panties," I say jokingly.

"Like I was saying," Paige continued, shooting me a playful yet dirty look, "It seemed like the perfect opportunity to snoop around. I'm wandering through the living room and kitchen; I look at photographs of him at family events and outings with friends – nothing alarming at first glance. So there I was, doing what we all secretly do – walking around, pretending to be pregnant, fantasizing about a future where this place is ours. I was imagining babies, parties, the whole nine yards."

I now take my eyes off the road for a second, look at Paige, and laugh. "I know you didn't say your ass was walking around fake pregnant." I couldn't stop laughing. "Girl, you have officially lost your mind," I say.

Paige joined me, laughing, "Don't act like you haven't done it! Now, stop making me laugh so I can finish telling you," Paige says. Her amusement was infectious, but she was obviously eager to return to her tale.

"Ok, carry on," I say.

"As I started to lose myself in this daydream, I was jolted back to reality by the sudden ring of a house phone in the bedroom. I know what you're about to say: Who the hell still has a house phone? Yes, he still has a house phone, complete with an answering machine."

I managed to suppress my laughter, letting her carry on with the story without interruption.

"Panic set in as I didn't want him to catch me snooping around. Girl, that damn answering machine became my unexpected knight in shining plastic as I let out a breath I didn't even know I was holding."

The answering machine clicked on: "You've reached Jacki and Devin; we're not in right now. Please leave your name and number at the beep, and we'll return your call as soon as possible. Beep."

Paige's voice was laced with disbelief as she recounted, "I just froze, utterly bewildered." Then the question hit me: *"Who the hell is Jacki? "*

Chapter Nine

As I tried to make sense of the situation, the caller's voice echoed from the answering machine, breaking my train of thought.

"Hey, Devin. It looks like you're out cold. I just wanted to tell you I'm not staying at my sister's. I'm just around the corner now, so I'll need your help with my bags when I arrive."

Suddenly, Devin's groggy voice responded from the machine, "Ah, bae, I'm here. Sorry, must've dozed off." There was a brief pause before he added, "Alright, give me a ring when you're at the door. See you soon. Bye."

I felt as if my feet were rooted to the floor, weighed down by shock. The next thing I knew, Devin was dashing down the hallway, wide-eyed and alert. Overwhelmed, I finally managed to speak. "What the hell, Devin?" My gaze dropped to see he was clutching my bag, packed with all my stuff.

"I can explain, but you need to get the hell out of here now." His tone was urgent, a stark contrast to his usual calm demeanor.

I snatched my bag, a mix of disgust and anger washing over me. "Get out? What do you mean, 'get out'? Where am I supposed to go? Remember, you're my ride back, you asshole!"

"Take the bus, damn it!" Devin shot back, his voice raised.

I pushed him, frustration boiling over. "Are you kidding me? There's no bus service from Spring to Hitchcock. What the hell is going on, Devin?"

His response was frantic, almost desperate. "Look, I know this is crazy, but you must hide in this closet right now. I'll get you out as soon as I can," he said, nudging me towards the closet in the living room.

I interrupted Paige's story, incredulous. "Hold on a second. You're telling me you actually let him shove your ass into a closet?"

Paige looked at me, her expression a mixture of aggravation and helplessness. "What else was I supposed to do? I was high as hell, confused as fuck, and for all I knew, this guy had a wife or a girlfriend who could be a bodybuilder or a martial arts expert. So yeah, I got my ass in that closet."

I couldn't help but burst into laughter again. "Why did your mind go straight to a bodybuilder?" I asked, laughing so hard that tears began streaming down my face.

"Bitch, can you stop laughing? You need to hear this; it gets way worse," Paige interjected, a serious tone cutting through her amusement. I mimed zipping my lips and nodded, signaling her to continue.

With a mix of reluctance and urgency, Paige recounted squeezing into the cramped, dark closet just as the front door swung open. "I could hear shuffling – that must've been his trifling ass, rushing to help this 'Jacki' person," she said.

She imitated Jacki's voice, laced with suspicion, "Why are you all out of breath?" Then, mimicking Devin's response, she said, "I was trying to hurry downstairs so you wouldn't have to carry everything."

"Girl, I was terrified," Paige admitted. "I'm rummaging through my bag as quietly as I can because, guess what, the closet I'm in has a full view of the living room. I'm searching for my phone to text you, only to remember I left it in his car last night in the heat of the moment."

She continued, "I could hear their conversation right outside the closet, and I was freaking out. Devin's trying to sound casual, asking Jacki why she didn't stay at her sister's another day. His ass sounded so damn awkward, and she definitely seemed to sense something was off. I barely breathed, trying to be as silent as possible in that closet."

As Paige described the tense exchange between Jacki and Devin, she suddenly realized how parched her mouth had become. "In the middle of all that chaos, I completely forgot about the blunt I'd smoked earlier. The effects were starting to kick in, and you know how dry my mouth gets," she said, her voice a mix of frustration and irony.

She recounted her desperate search in the bag for the small water bottle she usually carried, only to remember she'd taken it out to make space for her makeup. "Shit, I thought to myself," she muttered. "At this point, my eyes had finally adjusted to the dim light in the closet; I noticed a jacket in the closet with what looked like a bottle of water in its pocket. I managed to ease it out of the pocket quietly, but my relief turned to disgust when I realized it was a half-filled water bottle with an old doobie floating inside. Fuck my life!" she groaned.

"At this point, my mouth was a desert, devoid of any moisture, and it showed no signs of returning. I was so desperate that I said, "fuck it," and just went for it. I took a sip from that nasty bottle," Paige continued. "Girl, oh my god. That shit had been marinating for months and had acquired a taste of forgotten refrigerators and old weed."

I couldn't help but gag a little at the thought as Paige's narrative unfolded with each vivid, unfortunate detail.

"Meanwhile, Devin's attempts to distract Jacki were growing increasingly frantic. He suggested everything from a spontaneous breakfast to brunch, clearly trying to buy me an escape route.

But Jacki wasn't having any of it. So there I was, crammed in the closet, internally panicking and silently protesting. My phone was in his car, and the last thing I needed was for them to leave, only for Jacki to find it and the shit hit the fan or for Devin to discard it in a bid to cover his ass. Either way, I knew I was royally fucked!

Chapter Ten

When Jacki opted for a relaxed day in, I breathed a sigh of relief, thinking I might still have a chance to sneak out. Girl, I can't even begin to describe how many times I dozed off and woke up again. I felt like I was in solitary confinement, my sense of time completely warped, my sanity teetering on the edge in the darkness of that closet," Paige recounted.

"And then, as if things couldn't get worse, my bladder started protesting. You know, I've never been good at holding it in. Now shit got real as I desperately weighed my options. I tried crossing and uncrossing my legs, but it was no use. So, in a moment of sheer desperation, I made a quick, albeit regrettable, decision and grabbed the jacket from earlier. I couldn't use the towel I was wrapped in – I wasn't about to sit naked in that closet. I slid the jacket under me as quietly as possible, and I had no choice but to let go."

Paige continued, "This is where shit got crazy. The sound of liquid hitting fabric was unmistakable. I winced, praying it would go unnoticed. But little did I know that Devin and Jacki were right there in the living room.

'What the fuck was that?' I heard Jacki ask.

Devin's efforts to try and cover it up, saying it was probably the ice machine, failed miserably.

"That wasn't the damn ice machine. That came from the closet, and you need to get your ass up and check to make sure we don't have rats or something," Jacki said, annoyed.

"Girl, we don't have rats," Devin said dismissively.

When it became clear that Devin wasn't budging, she finally said, "I'll check it myself," with a snip and started heading my way."

Paige paused, a look of horror crossing her face. "When she said this, and I heard the footsteps get closer and closer, I think she scared my bladder because more pee started coming out.

I heard Devin trying to calm her down, but she was adamant about checking the closet.

"Why the fuck are you trying to keep me out of this closet, Devin?" Jacki growled.

At this point, they were standing right outside the closet door. Even though I couldn't see them, it was clear that the mood had changed from chill to full-on interrogation. Hell, my mood had changed in the closet, too.

At this moment, the door swung open, and there I was, face to face with Jacki.

She exploded at Devin, "What the fuck?! Who the fuck is this bitch?" as she started violently swinging at him.

While she was beating his ass, I quickly dressed and grabbed my bag and his car keys. I made a mad dash out the front door and down the stairs while frantically clicking the unlock button on his car. I flung open his car door, grabbed my phone, and ran to the front of the apartment complex. That's when I called you. And now, here we are."

I was utterly appalled. "Damn, girl! That shit sounds crazy as fuck! She didn't chase you or try to stop you?" I said, slightly surprised.

Paige shook her head. "No way was I sticking around to find out. I'm not about to get shot – I watch the news! Can we please grab some Whataburger? I need to get the taste of blunt water out of my mouth."

We both erupted into laughter. "You know damn well we're getting Whataburger," I said. Then, a sudden realization hit me. "Wait a minute; you sat your ass in my car after you pissed yourself?! Girl, you are getting my car detailed!"

What Ever Happened to Zoe Lane?

Zoe

Chapter Eleven

Like fine wine, a friendship often improve with time; ours is no exception. My tightly-knit circle, comprising Zoe, Marie, and myself, has been the cornerstone of my life since our high school days, weaving through the labyrinth of the past twenty years with strength and resilience.

Zoe's story is one marked by trials and triumphs. Her childhood was overshadowed by the turmoil of her parent's divorce when she was just six, a consequence of her father's struggles with alcohol and abusive behavior.

This upheaval led her mother, Loretta, to move Zoe and her brother from Dallas to Austin, a fresh start that, unfortunately, did little to mend the growing rift with her father. These early experiences shaped Zoe's perspective on family and relationships, a theme central to our story.

Our paths crossed in our sophomore year of high school, igniting a friendship that quickly blossomed into a bond as close as family. We were an inseparable trio, brimming with energy and humor, the highlight of every social gathering. Weekends were our realm, filled with laughter, impromptu dance-offs, and culinary escapades.

However, life has a way of intertwining joy with sorrow. In the latter part of our high school journey, Zoe's world was rocked by her mother's diagnosis of breast cancer. This challenge overshadowed our carefree days but also brought us closer together.

Transitioning to college, Zoe and I chose the University of Texas, embarking on a new chapter filled with academic pursuits and personal growth. At the same time, Marie set off for the University of Houston. Our friendship, though stretched across cities, remained unshaken.

Zoe and I, sharing a major in Psychology, kept each other motivated and focused while also exploring new relationships – Zoe with Eric, a classmate from her first-year biology course, and I with a Marine I had recently met during one of our weekend outings.

Tragically, the light of Zoe's life dimmed when her mother lost her brave fight against cancer at the end of our freshman year of college. The loss deeply affected Zoe, altering her once vibrant and optimistic nature. She grappled with her grief, her sense of direction faltering as her brother moved back to Dallas to be with their father.

Recognizing her need to get away, Marie and I planned a beach vacation to Destin, Florida, during our sophomore spring break. We hoped it would offer Zoe a much-needed break from the shadows that loomed over her.

The tension in the car was high as we drove, the usual banter and laughter conspicuously absent. Zoe seemed lost in thought; her usual spark dulled.

Marie's patience, already hanging by a thread, finally snapped, piercing the heavy silence. "Ok, I can't take it anymore! What's going on, Zoe?" she blurted out, her voice a turbulent blend of concern and frustration. "You've been miles away this whole trip!"

In my head, I couldn't help but think, 'Good Lord, Marie,' amazed at her directness yet understanding her need for answers.

Zoe's response, when it came, was a revelation that stunned us both: "I'm pregnant." The words hung in the air, heavy with implications and uncharted futures.

"Ok, not where I thought this was going," Marie said stunned.

I asked the inevitable, "Is Eric the father?" Zoe confirmed, yet he was unaware of the situation.
We sat in a reflective silence, each processing the gravity of Zoe's news. Her decision to keep the baby, which honored her mother's memory, spoke of her unwavering strength. She also revealed her plans to possibly move back to Dallas, seeking the support of her family there.

The trip to Destin took on a new significance; it was no longer just a vacation but a sanctuary from the storm awaiting

Zoe's return. As we neared New Orleans, we collectively let go of the weight of our worries, determined to make this getaway memorable.

Chapter Twelve

Spring Break was a reprieve from reality, a brief return to the carefree days of our high school years. The house we rented was a haven nestled by the sea, its walls echoing with the promise of laughter and the freedom of youth. From the moment we stepped through the door, the world's weight seemed to lift, replaced by an infectious excitement that reminded us of our high school days. We were again the inseparable trio, living in a bubble of joy and nostalgia.

Our days were a delightful blend of spontaneity and leisure. We indulged in local cuisine, savoring flavors that were as vibrant and diverse as our conversations. From fresh seafood to exotic local delicacies, every meal was an adventure in itself, creating a medley of tastes and shared experiences.

The evenings were a whirlwind of music and dance, each night a celebration of our reunion and a testament to our bond. We were the queens of the dance floor, our movements a reflection of our unspoken connection, each beat of the music echoing the heartbeat of our friendship.

As Spring Break drew to a close, a sense of melancholy intertwined with our contentment. Packing our bags, we were acutely aware that this retreat from reality was a rare gem, a precious memory in the making. The journey back was nostalgic; we were lost in thoughts of the days spent in laughter and the unspoken realization that life was about to resume its relentless pace.

Life has a funny way of sneaking up on you, as our return to Austin marked the end of an interlude to bliss and a harsh slap from reality, primarily for Zoe. I didn't think anything of it when I dropped Zoe off Thursday morning at her apartment, but Eric was waiting for her when we returned. Everything seemed fine, and he was his usual chipper self. However, the sense of foreboding I felt at the moment continued to linger through my errands that morning.

I had barely stepped into my house and dropped my bags when I got a frantic phone call from Zoe. "Whoa….slow down'" I urged, struggling to piece together her words through tears.

"Eric dumped me!" Zoe cried.

The news hit me like a freight train. "Honey…no. Did you tell him you were pregnant?" I said.

"I did, but I was explaining to him about moving back to Dallas to be closer to family, and he said he didn't want to do a long-distance relationship. I then told him about the baby, and he immediately said he wanted no part of that, threw $200 in my face, and said do what I need to before storming out."

I sat down slowly on the couch, shocked by what I had just heard. The cruelty of his departure, marked by a heartless gesture of throwing $200 at her, left me reeling in disbelief.

I quickly looped Marie into the call, knowing she would share our shock and anger. True to form, Marie's fiery spirit blazed. "Fuck that asshole!" she exclaimed, her protective instincts taking over. "Do you want me to key his car and slash his tires, or should I call my brothers? We can do all three, you know. How dare he treat you like this!" Her words, a mix of rage and concern, were of small comfort to Zoe, who continued to cry inconsolably. We spent the next hour on the phone, a triad of shared sorrow and frustration, offering words of support and solidarity to Zoe. The day passed in a blur, each hour a reminder of the stark reality that transpired.

That evening, another call from Zoe pierced the silence of my thoughts. She had decided to return to Dallas to seek refuge with her father and stepmother. The $200, a painful reminder of Eric's betrayal, was now her ticket to a new beginning. I agreed to drive her to the bus station without a second thought, my heart heavy with the knowledge that this could be our last goodbye.

The drive to the bus station was a journey of mixed emotions. Zoe sat beside me, determined to remain stoic, afraid of another emotional breakdown. We talked about everything and nothing, reminiscing about old times and sharing tentative hopes for the future. The bus station loomed ahead, a symbol of change and new beginnings.

As I helped Zoe with her bags, the finality of the moment settled in. Our goodbye was a silent promise of lasting friendship, a bond that distance and time could never erode. I watched as she boarded the bus, her figure gradually disappearing from view, leaving me with a sense of loss yet a fierce hope for her future.

In the days that followed, the absence of Zoe's presence was profound. The void she left was filled with memories and a quiet determination to stay connected, no matter the distance between us.

***

After Zoe's return to Dallas, her presence in our lives became like a distant echo. Our attempts to reach out were often met with brief, sporadic responses, just enough to let us know she and the baby were managing. The vibrant connection we once shared seemed to fade into a muted backdrop, leaving Marie and I in a state of concerned silence.

It was a surprise when Zoe's message broke through the quiet several months later. She was being induced in three days and wanted us by her side. Her request felt like a beacon in a fog, a sign that our bond, although weaker, still remained. Facing the judgmental views of her old-fashioned father on unwed motherhood, Zoe was reaching out for the support she sorely needed.

Unfortunately, neither of us could make it on such short notice. Determined to be there somehow, Marie and I did the next best thing: Skype!

Zoe's induction day arrived, showcasing Zoe's resolve and strength. Witnessing her bring new life into the world was nothing short of amazing. She navigated the waves of labor with elegance and ease. So it was fitting as Zoe cradled her newborn daughter; she would name her Grace, her mother's middle name.

Marie and I were enveloped in a warm glow, marveling at the newest member of our group, when suddenly, the atmosphere was shattered. Zoe's voice, laced with a sharp edge of anger, cut through the air like a knife. "What the fuck are you doing here?!" she demanded her tone a stark contrast to the serene scene we had just been admiring.

The abrupt shift from joyous celebration to tense confrontation jolted us, snapping our attention back to Zoe. Her eyes, previously soft with maternal affection, now blazed with a fierce intensity. The sudden change was disorienting, leaving Marie and me wide-eyed and bracing for what was to come.

Just beyond the camera's reach, a voice replied, "What do you mean?" In that instant, my instincts kicked in. Rising to my feet, I clutched the laptop, turning it this way and that in a futile attempt to alter Zoe's camera angle and catch a glimpse of the intruder. "GET OUT!" Zoe's voice thundered a harsh command that echoed through the room.

Marie's voice rose in urgency, "Zoe, who the hell is that? What's happening?" The hostility was detectable even through the screen.

The unseen visitor responded, eerily calm, "Now, is that any way to treat me? I know we didn't part on the best terms, but it's been so long." The voice was hauntingly familiar, sending a chill down my spine. Recognition dawned on me. "ZOE!" I exclaimed, my voice a mix of surprise and bewilderment, "Is that Eric? What the fuck is he doing there?"

Zoe's hand slowly moved the camera in that charged moment, quivering with anger and frustration. As the view shifted, it unveiled the startling image of Eric standing at the threshold of the delivery room. His sudden appearance, wholly unexpected and deeply unwelcome, tore through the sanctity of the moment like a dissonant note in a harmonious melody.

But the scene held yet another twist. Next to Eric was a woman, her presence casting a shadow of mystery and complication over the already strained atmosphere. She stood with a quiet poise that belied the turmoil around her. Her hair, a cascade of chestnut brown that fell gently to her shoulders, framed her face in a soft, almost artistic manner. Her eyes, a captivating green, seemed to dance between curiosity and unease as if she was acutely aware of the storm of emotions her presence had stirred.

She was dressed in a simple yet elegant blue dress that contrasted sharply with the sterile backdrop of the hospital room. Her hands were clasped together, perhaps subconsciously to comfort herself amid the unfolding drama. Despite her poised appearance, there was an undeniable unease about her, as if she was suddenly questioning the decision to accompany Eric to this most private and delicate of moments.

Her unexpected and unexplained presence hung in the air like an unanswered question, adding to the surreal nature of the scene unfolding before our eyes.

Unable to contain her outrage, Marie shouted, "Oh, HELL NO! What the hell is he doing there, and who's that woman with him?" Her words echoed my own feelings of disbelief and outrage.

I could feel my blood simmering with anger, a mere reflection of the storm of emotions Zoe must have been experiencing. In a moment of clarity amidst the chaos, Zoe called for the nurse, gently handing her newborn daughter, Grace, back into her arms. Her request for a few minutes alone was laced with a quiet strength.

The nurse, sensing the delicacy of the situation, cast a lingering, scrutinizing glance at Eric. There was apprehension in her movements as she placed Grace in the bassinet and began to exit the room, her eyes never leaving Eric. The door closed behind her with a soft click, leaving Zoe to confront the ghosts of her past, now standing uninvited in her presence.

Eric tentatively stepped closer to Zoe's bedside, his movements hesitant as he reached for the edge of the bed. Yet, he paused mid-action, halted by the piercing glare Zoe directed at him, a silent warning that spoke louder than words. He straightened, opting to maintain a respectful distance.

"Look, I know I was an asshole when we last spoke, but I ran into your brother at the Austin Food and Wine Festival last weekend. He told me about the induction, about our daughter..." His words trailed off as Zoe cut him off sharply.

"Our daughter?" Zoe's voice was a blend of surprise and anger. "You threw money at me as if I was nothing, then shut me out of your life completely. And now you talk of 'our daughter'?"

Eric's expression shifted, a flicker of remorse passing over his face. "I know I messed up terribly. I was wrong. But I've changed. I want to be there for Grace, to support her in any way possible."

It was then that the woman at the door, the enigma who had silently observed the unfolding drama, spoke up. "Yes, we do," she said softly.

Marie's response was immediate and fiery. "Bitch, nobody asked you!" she yelled.

"Marie!" I hissed through clenched teeth, trying to temper her outburst. Under my breath, I couldn't help but mutter, "But she does have a point."

Eric, clearly frustrated, rolled his eyes and moved toward the woman at the door, taking her hand. "My fiancée, Emma, and I don't want to cause any trouble," he said, his tone shifting to one of forced calmness. "I just wanted to see the baby and request a paternity test to confirm she's mine. You owe me at least this."

A burst of laughter involuntarily escaped my lips as I watched Marie, ever the dramatic, slide off her chair and onto the floor, her reaction a perfect embodiment of the absurdity unfolding before us. My hand flew to my mouth in an attempt to stifle further giggles, but the amusement quickly faded as I noticed Zoe's expression, a fire brewing in her eyes.

"You know, Eric," Zoe began, her voice chillingly calm, starkly contrasting the flurry of emotions swirling within her. "You have some nerve showing up here after seven months, parading around with your new... flavor of the month and preaching about change. I don't owe you anything."

Emma, the previously silent observer, stepped forward, her voice tinged with nervous conviction. "He has a right to know. It's only fair," she asserted, though her uncertainty was apparent.

Zoe's response was a laugh, but it was devoid of humor. It was the kind of laugh that sent shivers down your spine and signaled a breaking point. Marie and I exchanged a glance, a silent understanding passing between us. We braced ourselves, knowing all too well that when calm follows rage in such quick succession, the fallout is imminent.

Zoe harbored no doubts about Eric's paternity of Grace; that truth was as clear to her as the day. Yet, she also understood a more profound, unsaid reality: the results of any paternity test would change nothing in the grand scheme of their fractured relationship. Eric's flight in the face of responsibility foreshadowed his likely actions now, regardless of his hollow claims of transformation. Deep down, Zoe knew that the tides of change, no matter how earnestly sworn, rarely turned in the hearts of those who had once chosen to run.

"Ok, Eric... let's do the paternity test," Zoe said, her words laced with a challenge, a clear 'bring it on' in her tone.

Chapter Thirteen

After Eric unceremoniously rained on our parade, Marie and I thought it best to give Zoe some space to recuperate. We wanted her to process and recover from the day's emotional rollercoaster. The following day, in a scene somewhat reminiscent of a daytime soap opera, Zoe and Eric underwent the DNA test at the hospital. Those next days dragged on, each of us suspended in a state of anxious anticipation for the results.

Finally, the moment of truth arrived. Zoe called me; her voice, tinged with anxiety, echoed through the phone. "I can't bring myself to open this email," she confessed.

"Why not? I thought Eric was a shoo-in for Daddy of the Year," I quipped, trying to lighten the mood.

"I don't know. What if things change? What if…?" Zoe trailed off, leaving a pregnant pause.

"What if Eric's not the father?" I ventured, my curiosity piqued but sensing this wasn't the time for an interrogation. I could already feel this conversation was spiraling into a vortex of indecision.

"Yeah," she sighed, sounding deflated.

Confused, I responded, "But I thought you were certain Eric was the father?"

Her voice snapped with a hint of irritation, "I know what the fuck I said."

I decided to rally my inner cheerleader. "Zoe, weren't you Ms. Independent about this whole thing? Remember, 'Eric or no Eric, I've got this'? Time to channel that boss bitch energy and face those results. You've got this!"

After several moments of hesitation, she replies, "You're right," her tone shifting from uncertain to determined.

As I tried to navigate this emotional minefield, my boyfriend gave me the "We're going to miss the movie" death glare. I signaled for five more minutes, but Zoe cut through the silent argument. "He's the father," she announced, her voice a mix of relief and something else I couldn't quite place.

I was momentarily distracted by my boyfriend's insistence, and it took me a moment to refocus. "That's great, Zoe. But are you ok with this?" There was a silence on the other end before Zoe abruptly said, "Let me call you back," and hung up.

I stared at my phone for a second, thinking, "Rude much!" but inevitably, I was left pondering her reaction. Did she have lingering feelings for Eric? Was she hoping for a different outcome?

As I spilled the beans to Marie the following day, her reaction was priceless. "STOP! Girl, this is too much tea for the morning! I am still trying to process my own reality!" she exclaimed. I confessed how distracted I'd been during the movie, my thoughts consumed by Zoe's situation.

After much deliberation and several wild theories later, we decided to confront Zoe. When we finally got her on the phone, the sounds of Grace and Eric cooing in the background greeted us.

"Zoe, what's happening?" I asked, trying to piece together the puzzle.

"Oh, hey!" she replied, caught off guard. "Can I…"

Marie interjected before she could defer the conversation, "No, you most certainly cannot."

"Fine, let me go in the bedroom. Hang on," the annoyance clear in her tone.

Zoe was back after some muffled exchanges and the sound of a door closing. "Hello?" she said, her voice weary.

"So," Marie began, sounding like a detective about to crack a case, "What's going on?"

"Nothing, just spending time with Grace," Zoe replied nonchalantly.

"Where's Emma?" I prodded, my suspicion growing.

"How should I know?" Zoe retorted with distinct irritation.

Marie and I couldn't help but chorus in unison, "ZOE!"

I cut to the chase, "Look, this whole situation with Eric smells like trouble. He's got a fiancée, remember?"

"He's just being a dad," Zoe defended, but it was clear to Marie and me that she was wading into dangerous waters, her fantasies about Eric clouding her judgment.

The conversation spun in circles, with Zoe's stubborn optimism clashing against our pragmatic warnings. It became evident that Zoe was entangled in her own fantasy, seeing Grace as a potential bridge to reconcile with Eric. Eventually, Marie and I realized we were hitting a brick wall. We agreed to weekly phone check-ins, dubbing them 'Spill-the-Tea Fridays,' hoping Zoe would come to her senses before the next dramatic twist in her soap opera life unfolded.

Chapter Fourteen

As Grace neared her first birthday, our little circle had witnessed a whirlwind of changes. Marie and I were basking in the glow of recent engagements, and my college graduation was just on the horizon. In stark contrast, Zoe's life seemed to orbit entirely around Grace and, inexplicably, Eric. Despite his wedding to Emma being mere weeks away, Zoe and Eric appeared more entangled than ever. Each Spill-the-Tea Friday, Zoe regaled us with tales of their escapades, blissfully unaware of the foolishness of it all. She even casually said they were invited to Eric's wedding, with Grace participating in the ceremony. On the other end of the line, Marie and I had to exercise Herculean restraint, pretending to cheer while foreseeing the inevitable train wreck approaching. My grandmother's words echoed in my mind, "A hard head makes for a soft ass," never more apt than in this saga.

The week before Eric's nuptials, I was unloading groceries when Marie's call came through, her tone laden with the 'I-told-you-so' news we'd been dreading. Depositing the groceries haphazardly, I braced myself for the inevitable. "Hold on," she said, and the line was suddenly filled with Zoe's muffled sobs. Internally groaning, I grabbed a water bottle and retreated to my bedroom, preparing for the emotional deluge.

"Zoe, sweetie, what happened?" I asked, met with an intensification of her sobs.

Marie, equally frustrated, revealed her unsuccessful attempts to coax the story out of her. Deciding on a tough-love approach, I pressed, "Zoe, we can't help if you don't talk. What the hell happened?"

Marie's shocked "Damn, girl!" was met with my impatient, "Well?"

After gathering her composure, Zoe lamented, "I don't get it. How could he do this to us again?"

"Eric?" Marie and I asked in unison, already knowing the answer.

Zoe recounted the morning's events. Eric, usually jovial during his visits, was noticeably somber. "I can't do this anymore, Zoe," he declared cryptically.

Zoe, her mind a maze of confusion, demanded clarity from Eric. His admission struck her like a lightning bolt – his guilt over their secret liaisons was eating him alive, especially now that Emma was carrying his child. Eric, seemingly committed to right his past wrongs, had confessed everything to Emma, and in a turn of events that bordered on the unbelievable, she had chosen to stand by him. This revelation meant one heart-wrenching reality for Zoe: Eric was severing ties with her and Grace.

Zoe's world spun as she processed his words. "I can't do this anymore, Zoe," Eric had said, his voice heavy with a decisiveness that chilled her to the bone.

"Do what?" she had asked, playing coy and slowly unbuttoning her shirt.

"All of this," Eric had gestured, encompassing the little world they had built together.

Zoe, realizing the seriousness of the conversation, backed away and sat on the edge of the couch. Desperation began seeping into her voice. "You mean spending time with me and your daughter?"

Eric's response was a brutal blow. "And that's exactly the problem. It's not just about seeing Grace. We've been….sleeping together. And I can't look Emma in the eye because of it."

The sternness of his tone made Zoe recoil, her heart sinking. "Emma is pregnant. We found out this morning. I've got a chance to do things right this time," Eric declared, his words cutting through Zoe like a knife.

"What the fuck does that mean, Eric? I was just a learning curve or something?" Zoe's voice had cracked, a mixture of rage and offense coloring her words.

"I've changed, Zoe. I meant it. But I can't see you anymore," Eric had said, his voice firm yet strained.

Zoe's mind raced, trying to grasp the strands of her unraveling life. "What about Grace? She needs her father!"

Eric's following words had been a crushing finality. "I can't see her either. It's the only way."

"Is this what Emma wants?" Zoe had asked, her voice laced with accusation.

"No, Zoe. This is my decision," Eric had stated, the resolve in his voice leaving no room for negotiation.

As Eric had moved towards the door, Zoe's pleas grew more frantic. "You can't just walk out on us again," she had begged.

Eric had paused, his hand on the doorknob as if wrestling with his conscience. But then, with a sigh that felt like the closing of a chapter, he stepped out and closed the door behind him, leaving Zoe in a shattered silence.

***

As the silence on the phone stretched uncomfortably, Marie and I struggled to restrain ourselves from voicing the inevitable "I told you so." The tension was evident, almost comical, as if we were characters in a sitcom waiting for the cue to deliver our punchline. But we held back, waiting for Zoe to break the ice. The wait, however, stretched on endlessly.

Finally, Marie, notorious for her aversion to uncomfortable silences, ventured into the fray. "Well, maybe this is for the best, you know." Her words, meant to soothe, instead ignited a fire.

Zoe's reaction was immediate and fierce. "What the fuck is that supposed to mean?" she snapped back, her voice bristling with hostility.

"Whoa!" I exclaimed, taken aback by the intensity of her response. "Let's just take a second here before we say things we will regret."

Still reeling from Zoe's biting comeback, Marie sputtered, "I'm sorry...what?!" But her tone was more incredulous than apologetic.

Zoe, now fully unleashed, let her frustration pour out. "You fucking heard me! How is being a single mother for the best? So only you two get to have fairy-tale lives while I'm stuck in Grimm's fucking nightmare?"

I knew Zoe was taking her anger out on us, but I could sense the situation going left in 3, 2, 1...

"This bitch has some nerve to come at me with an attitude. Playing happy families with your engaged baby daddy was never going to have a storybook ending. Were you expecting to ride off into the sunset together?" Marie countered, never one to back down.

Zoe's laugh was tinged with bitterness. "Oh, right, because I'm the blueprint for disaster! Just because you're on cloud nine with your engagements doesn't mean you're immune to life throwing a curveball. You are just as fucked up as I am!"

Marie's retort cut deep. "Ah yes...because I'm dumb enough to let a man leave me twice. But sure, go on, play the martyr."

"Alright, that's enough!" I interjected, feeling like I was between two siblings having a knock-down, drag-out fight. "You both are just lashing out now. We are getting nowhere like this."

But Zoe was far from done. "Shut the fuck up!" she yelled through the phone, her anger now aimed at me. "You think you're so high and mighty. Well, welcome to the real world, where life can be an absolute shit-show. You think you are so damn perfect prancing around like a fucking Barbie! You make me sick!"

I shot back, feeling my own temper flare, "What's your fucking problem, Zoe? You're the one who walked into this mess with your eyes wide open. When we tried to tell you this whole thing was a bad idea, you treated us like we were the crazy ones. Now that this shit has blown up in your face don't drag us down with your regrets!"

Her reply was a calm "Noted," followed by the abrupt end of the call.

Stunned, I asked into the void, "What the fuck just happened?" Marie's voice, heavy with frustration and sadness, came through. "Zoe's gone off the deep end. She's playing the victim, but she's been screwing Eric this whole time, and she expects me to feel sorry for her now?"

Marie sighed heavily, "I can't deal with this shit anymore. She's made her bed, now she can lie in it. I need a break. I'll call you later," and with that, she hung up.

I laid in bed, my mind racing, replaying the explosive call. Our trio, once inseparable, now seemed irreparably torn apart.

Attempts to reach Zoe were futile; she had changed her number, cutting off any chance of reconciliation. As the days blended into weeks and weeks stretched into months and years, the bond between Marie and me remained as strong as ever. Three years had flown by, ushering in a multitude of life changes – both Marie and I had walked down the aisle, and now, I was eagerly awaiting the arrival of my first child. In quiet moments, my thoughts would drift to Zoe and little Grace. I wondered how they were faring, but with no means to reach Zoe, those thoughts remained unanswered.

On a sunny afternoon, just as Marie and I were finishing a leisurely lunch and about to embark on a baby shopping spree, my phone rang with an unknown number flashing on the screen. Curiously, I answered, "Hello," while gathering our things from the table.

The line crackled with heavy, labored breathing, punctuated by the distant sound of a man's voice, raised in anger. "Hello?" I repeated, my brow furrowing in confusion. Marie's eyes were filled with questions at my side as she watched me intently.

Shrugging, I switched the phone to speaker, giving Marie a glimpse into the mysterious call. "Hello?" I called out again, my finger hovering over the 'end call' button, ready to dismiss it as a prank.

Just then, a voice, frail and trembling, barely rose above a whisper, "Please don't hang up." The desperation in the caller's voice was unmistakable.

Marie and I exchanged a look of dawning realization — we knew that voice. "Zoe..." I breathed, my heart skipping a beat.

Marie leaned in closer, her expression a blend of concern and surprise. The background noise grew louder for a moment, the sound of shouting more distinct, before fading away as if someone had moved to a quieter place.

"Zoe, is that you? What's going on? Are you ok?" My voice was laced with worry, the joyful anticipation of baby shopping forgotten in an instant.

There was a pause, filled with the kind of heavy silence that speaks volumes, before Zoe's voice came through again, quivering with emotion. "I need help," she whispered, her words sending a chill down my spine.

Potions and Pickles

Katie

Chapter Fifteen

If you had told me a few years ago that I would be chronicling the saga of my friend Katie and her scandalous suburban escapades, I would have burst into laughter, martini splashing over the rim. Yet, life has a peculiar knack for dishing out unforeseen twists, the kind you never knew you were missing. Brace yourself, for I'm about to unravel how Sunshine Meadows transformed into a real-life sitcom that would make even Hollywood envious.

It all started innocently enough—or as innocent as an affair can be, I suppose. Katie and her neighbor, Terry, seemed an unlikely pair. Katie was the embodiment of a free spirit. Being an artist allowed her to view life as a vast canvas awaiting bold, unbridled strokes. Katie embraced her radiant melanin skin and voluptuous figure that emanated raw confidence. She proudly wore her natural, curly black hair in large afro puffs like a wild crown, accentuating her fierce individuality. Her husband James, a high school science teacher, was her polar opposite, his strait-laced nature balancing her impulsive spirit.

Terry on the other hand, was Mr. Perfect Suburbia with lawns manicured to precision, a golfing enthusiast, his life was a clockwork of mundane predictability. But oh, was he a sight - a vision with piercing blue eyes radiated a mesmerizing allure as if the irises were a window into a world of passion and excitement. His presence was commanding, and that rendered him irresistible. And Katie, she was not immune.

Hell, even I, hearing her descriptions, found myself enticed by the idea of him. How Katie described Terry made it hard to believe he was a buttoned-up accountant tethered to a wife named Emily.

How on earth did these two completely different people end up in an affair? Well, it's funny you should ask – at the time, they were oblivious, but they had three shared interests: a strong desire for sex, a liking for recreational drugs, and, believe it or not, the same damn drug dealer. Can you believe the odds?

***

Not particularly in the mood for a night out, Terry entered the house party, only there to collect a new pack from his friend and occasional drug dealer, Nate. As he observed the unfamiliar faces gathered, he realized the past week had been exhausting. Terry had been dealing with an increasing workload and constant arguments with his wife about starting a family. Despite Terry's eagerness to become a father, his wife, Emily, stood firm in her decision not to have children.

Terry struggled to understand Emily's reluctance, and when questioned, she simply stated that kids had never been in her plans. Despite his deep desire to be a father, Terry suppressed his dream, prioritizing his love for Emily over his own desires. Feeling the weight of a particularly stressful week, when Terry got the call from Nate asking him to come by his little soiree, he thought, 'What the hell?!' He could use some new smoke, and Nate's party typically had some interesting choices in party favors.

Accustomed to his solitary existence, Terry rarely ventured beyond his social group, consisting mainly of co-workers and the dull crowd his wife would invite over every other weekend for tedious dinner parties. But unlike those events, tonight's vibe was real chill; something about this evening felt different. Standing at the bar, absorbed in his thoughts and casually scanning the room for Nate, Terry observed a woman on the dance floor. Her eyes were fixed on his as she swayed her hips to the music. Terry couldn't help but think she looked familiar, wearing a smile that seemed to illuminate the room. Terry kept his eyes on her as she moved gracefully with the rhythm, her curvy figure flowing smoothly as she maintained eye contact with Terry.

The woman strolled towards him, and Terry could feel his heart rate quicken – she was stunning. She was short in stature, which Terry amusingly found charming and attractive. Her chocolate brown skin exuded a warm glow as she approached. Without saying a word, she extended her hand towards him. Terry gently placed his hand on top of hers, entranced by her sweet smile. – though he briefly wondered if it was the smoky haze that filled the room. She led him to the makeshift dance floor and turned to press her body close to his. She started dancing, her hips swayed rhythmically, in sync with his movements. Terry couldn't recall the last time he danced like this, if ever. She leaned her head back, looking up at him, "You're Terry, right?" she asked.

Terry nodded, "Yes." With a clearer view, Terry recognized her. "I know you. You're Katie from two houses down, aren't you?" he said.

She smiled, a playful edge to her voice, "Good memory, Terry, from two houses down."

Terry could tell she was slightly tipsy as she slurred her words, but too caught up in the moment, he continued to dance.

"What are you doing here? This doesn't seem like a party you would attend?" she asked, taking Terry's hands and slowly guiding them along the sides of her body onto her hips.

Terry jokingly responded, "And here I was, thinking Katie from two houses down was the nicest person around, and now she's judging me by my cover."

Their laughter mingled in the air. Still swaying to the music, Katie faced him and apologized, "I didn't mean any offense."

"No offense taken," Terry assured her with a smile. "But you're right, this isn't my typical scene. I'm here looking for my friend Nate."

"Wait, you know Nate?" Katie said, surprised.

"You know Nate, too? Terry asked, delighted at the coincidence.

Katie nodded. "Oh, I've known Nate all my life, since middle school days."

Terry raised an eyebrow, intrigued. "Small world."

"Yeah," Katie agreed, suddenly remarking, "It's hot in here, isn't it? Let's grab a drink," she suggested, leading the way to the bar.

As Terry and Katie made their way to the bar, Nate appeared, greeting them warmly. "Hey, Terry. I'm glad you could join us! And I see you've met Katie, my sister from another mister."

Katie playfully shoved Nate, teasing, "Where have you been hiding?"

"Just setting up some games for tonight's fun," Nate replied, casually twirling a curl of Katie's hair. He then produced a gigantic blunt, so large that both Terry and Katie were surprised by its size. Nate dubbed it "The Crossbow," announcing to everyone that tonight's party would feature a smoking game instead of the usual drinking game.

With a mischievous grin, Nate laid out the rules. Terry and Katie, already paired up, found themselves designated as Team 3, scheduled to be the third in line. As Nate lit the Crossbow and handed it to the first team, a fragrant haze began to envelop the room. Excitement and laughter filled the air as the smoking game commenced.

Terry gave Katie a look that mixed surprise and amusement. "Well, this is definitely not my typical night," he joked.

Katie chuckled in response, "Tell me about it. But hey, why not enjoy the unexpected?" As they awaited their turn, Terry and Katie exchanged playful glances, both curious about where the night might lead.

As the night progressed, Terry and Katie found themselves immersed in the insane smoking game, leaving them high-five Jesus high. Laughter echoed through the room as various teams competed, but Terry and Katie's team emerged victorious, outlasting everyone else.

Terry and Katie found themselves among the few remaining guests as the party winded down. Walking together to Katie's car, they shared laughs and joked about the night's unexpected twists. Having finally reached her car, the conversation flowed effortlessly, the connection between them growing deeper.

Terry watched Katie as she spoke and, without thinking, leaned in to kiss her. Katie initially stepped back, prompting Terry to apologize. Before he could utter a word, Katie grabbed his shirt, pulling him towards her, reciprocating the kiss. When they finally parted, they shared a lingering gaze as Katie spoke first, attempting to break the silence. "Well, that just happened," she said.

Terry chuckled nervously, "Yeah, it sure did."

Their gazes locked; Terry gently tugged Katie closer by the loops of her jeans. "So, what do we do about it?" he asked, a hint of curiosity in his voice.

Without hesitation, they exchanged numbers, and from that moment on, they couldn't get enough of each other.

Chapter Sixteen

Terry and Katie were an odd couple, drawn together as if they had conjured each other without rational explanation. Their secret rendezvous were like something straight out of a spy novel - Terry sneaking into Katie's art studio under the veil of night, their trysts in motels disguised as business trips. But in Sunshine Meadows, secrets have a way of surfacing, and their affair was no exception. The local gossip machine was ever potent, yet they seemed adept at the game of deceit. Unbeknownst to them, their intricate web of lies was on the brink of a disastrous unraveling in the most absurd way possible.

One day, after an especially "creative" afternoon, Terry and Katie were basking in the afterglow when he turned to her with a mischievous glint in his eyes. He presented Katie with a mysterious vial of iridescent liquid. "What's this, Terry? A love potion? Are we turning Shakespearean now?" Katie joked, eyeing the vial skeptically. "You know, Katie, life is all about taking risks. Why not live a little dangerously?" Terry chuckled. "What's the worst that could happen?"

Famous last words, right?!

Katie, usually cautious, was swept up in the moment, and they both plunged headfirst into the unknown, consuming the potion like it was mere candy. It turned out to be a potent hallucinogenic, said to be similar to taking mushrooms with a splash of acid and ecstasy.

The effects of the enchanting potion cast an immediate spell upon them, catapulting them into an otherworldly realm of passion. Their eyes locked, becoming deep pools of ever-shifting color, promising unspoken desire and pleasure. Each caress sent sparks as they touched, igniting trails of warmth and electric tingles that echoed through their bodies.

Terry stared at Katie, obsessed with her beauty. He moved a fallen strand of hair from her face before slowly trailing his finger down to her neck and circling it around her right nipple. Katie's body responded in kind as her nipples immediately hardened at Terry's light and teasing touch. Katie reached for Terry, pulling him into her and kissing him deeply. For a moment, they seemed to meld into one; their heart rates quickened with each kiss and playful bite of each other's lips.

Terry, unable to control himself and longing for more, began to trail kisses down Katie's chest and stomach, stopping just before her sweet spot. Katie, writhing in anticipation, gasped, "Terry, what are you doing? Why are you stopping?"

"I want to hear you beg for me. Tell me how badly you want me to taste you. Tell me you are mine," Terry said with a commanding tone.

Katie, now out of her mind, a mix of the potion and the sexual tension building, could barely focus, let alone form words. She could feel Terry's breath right at her clitoris, teasing her, beckoning her to give into his control. A breathy whisper escaped Katie's mouth. "I'm yours to do with as you please."

Terry's wicked smile returned, and he began to greedily lick and suck at Katie's clit. He traced a pattern with his tongue as he moved Katie's leg over his shoulder, drawing her closer to him. Katie's breathing, now short, shallow breaths, ran her fingers through his hair, grinding her hips into his face, bringing herself closer to the edge. She could feel Terry's hands massaging her breasts and pinching her nipples as he licked and sucked away below. The combination of everything had Katie swirling in unbridled lust and yearning. As Katie felt her orgasm drawing close, Terry stopped, saying, "Not yet."

Katie, confused and horny, was finding the words to protest but struggling as a result of the effects of the potion; she felt Terry's hand grab a fistful of her hair and pull as he thrust his hard cock into the wetness of her pussy. They both moaned as his entire length was enveloped inside of her. With each thrust, moans of pleasure would escape from their lips as their bodies became one. Katie wrapped her legs around Terry, quickening the pace and tightening her essence around his member. Terry, lost in the feeling of Katie's sex, moved his hand to Katie's neck, pulling her to him so he could taste her mouth on his.

Breathless, Terry exclaims, "Shit, Katie, you feel fucking amazing."

"I know," she confidently said as she rolled on top of him, not missing a beat. She began riding him hard and fast. She could feel Terry's nails run down her back before he smacked her ass, causing her to cry out in surprise and delight. Katie moved Terry's hands to her breasts. As he squeezed, she said, "I want you to cum deep inside of me. I want all of you."

Terry wrapped his arms around her as he pulled her forward and began thrusting deep and quick. They could both feel their orgasms near as the room melted around them, swirling with iridescent hues that appeared to dance to the rhythm of their lovemaking. The boundaries between them blurred, and the very air was charged with their shared heartbeat.

"Fuck," Terry yelled out as he came deep inside of Katie, sending Katie over the edge, overcome by her own orgasm that seemed to last forever. Katie lay on Terry's chest, unable to move as each attempt ignited sparks in both of them, an apparent result of the potion ingested earlier.

As they rest in euphoric bliss, time seemed to lose its grip, each moment stretching into infinity. The happiness they felt in that moment ruled supreme, and the outside world's sounds faded into a distant whisper as sleep swept over them. They surrendered to its embrace, content in each other's arms.

A few weeks had passed, and life seemed to march on as usual. Katie and Terry's affair was at its highest point. Until one fateful day, Katie felt an inexplicable craving for pickles—yes, pickles. Now, Katie has never been one to obsess over food, but suddenly, pickles were all she could think about. She found herself at the grocery store, surrounded by jars of pickles of all shapes and sizes.

In a pickle daze, Katie began hoarding every jar she could get her hands on, as if possessed by the spirit of a pickle connoisseur. Nobody knew this seemingly harmless pickle binge would turn their whole world upside down.

***

One evening, as Terry and Katie indulged in their usual rendezvous, she blurted out her newfound obsession with pickles. Terry, always the rational one, suggested they indulge in her cravings, thinking it was just a passing phase. So, there they were, surrounded by an assortment of pickles, and I'm not even going to get into the crazy shit they did with these pickles; you have an imagination, so use it.

In the midst of them, lying in bed at one of their favorite hotels, smoking a joint, Terry looked at Katie wide-eyed like a bolt from out of the blue. "What if you're pregnant?" he said. The word 'pregnant' echoed through the room, a jolt of reality shattering their illicit bubble.

Katie's eyes widened in sudden realization, the bizarre puzzle pieces coming together - the love potion, the insane sex they had on the potion, and now the absurd obsession with pickles. She leaped out of bed, her voice a mix of panic and disbelief, "Oh fuck!"

Terry, caught off guard by her sudden outburst, could only stare back, his expression a portrait of confusion. "Terry?!" Katie says a little louder. "Aren't you on birth control?" Terry asks apprehensively. Katie stopped in her tracks, turning to face him. Her response was straightforward yet laden with the weight of the implications, "Uh, no!"

The absurdity escalated as they found themselves in a CVS bathroom, anxiously waiting for a pregnancy test result. ***Positive. WTF!***

The test showed two unmistakable lines, and suddenly, their affair was no longer a fling—it was a ticking time bomb. "Get more tests, Terry! This can't be right!" Katie's voice was laced with panic. "Go get more right now!" she barked at Terry. "This can't be happening!" Katie says as the severity of the situation set in.

Ten pregnancy tests later, each confirming the inevitable, they were forced to face the reality of their situation. Terry and Katie stared at the positive pregnancy tests in stunned silence. The air in the hotel room felt charged with a mix of anxiousness and sheer terror. They exchanged wide-eyed glances, the weight of their secret affair suddenly crashing down on them like a tidal wave.

Once a quirky backdrop to an unconventional love story, the pickle jars that surrounded them now seemed like silent witnesses to a situation that had spiraled out of control.

Terry, usually the epitome of composure, was a picture of distress, pacing the room, running his hands through his neatly combed hair in a gesture of nervous agitation. "Katie, what are we going to do? This is... it's insane! We're both married! This is a whole new level of disaster! Why aren't you on birth control?"

His words hung in the air, the reality of their predicament sinking in as they grappled with the daunting prospect of impending parenthood amid tangled relationships. Once a source of amusement, the pickles now seemed like a metaphor for the sour pickle they had found themselves in.

"Katie, say something!" Terry called out, voice raised. Katie couldn't think of a time she had ever heard him raise his voice. Nervously, she answered barely above a whisper, "I thought I couldn't get pregnant." Katie sat on the bed in shock.

"What did you say?" Terry asked, sitting next to her.

As they grappled with the reality of the pregnancy, a profound heaviness enveloped the room like a dense fog of uncertainty and fear. In this moment of vulnerability, Katie summoned the strength to unveil a profoundly personal truth she had held close to her heart. Her voice, quivering with a blend of sadness and disbelief, broke the silence.

"Terry," she began, her words laced with a noticeable mix of fear and resignation, "I never imagined this could happen. For years, James and I have been trapped in a silent battle with infertility. We've endured endless cycles of treatments, tests, and hope, only to be met with disappointment each time. The doctors, they were baffled - they found no reason, no explanation for our struggles."

Katie paused, collecting her thoughts, her gaze distant as if reliving every moment of that journey. "It became our unspoken sorrow, a chapter of our lives marked by its absence. We had come to accept, perhaps even mourn, that parenthood might not be our destiny. The dream of holding our child seemed a beautiful yet unreachable notion."

Terry's eyes widened with understanding and shock. The revelation added another layer of complexity to their already convoluted situation. The fertility struggles that James and Katie had faced suddenly became a poignant backdrop to the unexpected joy and chaos that their affair had unleashed. The irony of Katie's newfound fertility, coupled with the secret nature of their relationship, hung heavily in the air, leaving both grappling with the profound implications of the life-altering news.

Staring at each other amid the revelation, Terry and Katie found themselves at a crossroads, uncertain of the next steps. The room, once filled with fun, lust, and adventure, was now a sad reminder of the mistakes made.

After a moment of shared silence, Terry took a deep breath, his usually confident demeanor wavering. "Katie," he began slowly, "We need to face this together. It's complicated, but we can't ignore it. We owe it to ourselves and, more importantly, to this unborn child to figure out a plan. We must talk to our spouses, be honest about the situation, and navigate the consequences together."

"Whoa, Terry, let's not get ahead of ourselves," Katie began, her voice tinged with caution. "This is complicated. If this baby is yours, we have a responsibility to our partners and the child to be honest. But I've been trying for a baby with my husband. I need to see a doctor first to figure out the timeline before we potentially cause more pain. Telling them about our affair is hard enough without the added bombshell of a pregnancy. We don't need things to turn into a Jerry Springer episode."

Terry sat quietly on the bed, contemplating Katie's words. "So, what, we're going to wait until the baby's born?" he asked, his voice edged with a sharpness Katie hadn't heard before. "Katie, I think your husband might notice his black son or daughter coming out with fair skin and blue eyes. It's going to be pretty obvious. We can't just pretend nothing's wrong and hope for the best. The longer we wait, the messier it'll get."

Katie rose from the bed and found a spot on the floor between Terry's legs, gently pulling him to sit behind her. He enveloped her in his arms, and she nestled her head against his chest, pausing momentarily before speaking. "I'm not suggesting we wait indefinitely. First, we need to understand what we're dealing with. These past months with you have been incredible, unlike anything I've experienced. But we need to think this through. Are we both prepared to leave our spouses? I can't honestly say I'm ready to leave my husband. We haven't talked about the future; it's been all about getting high and having sex. Let's not rush into anything until I see the doctor. We should avoid causing more hurt than necessary."

Terry responded by tightening his embrace and gently kissing her forehead. "Okay," he agreed softly. "You're right. We'll face this when we have all the facts. For now, let's be cautious and think things through. We can't take chances like we did. Everything has to be smooth if this is going to work, okay?"

Katie stood up, a sense of resolution in her voice. "I agree. I need to head home. James will be back in about an hour." She leaned in and shared a tender kiss with Terry. "I'll text you once I'm home," she promised. Terry returned her kiss, a silent understanding passing between them. He watched as she collected her things and left.

Chapter Seventeen

Two weeks later.....

Katie anxiously paced her cozy art studio, contemplating what to occupy her mind with as she awaited her impending doctor's appointment. The vibrant colors around her seemed to swirl into a frenzied blur, reflecting the chaos in her heart. It was a familiar feeling of being lost, reminiscent of the heartache she and James experienced over their fertility struggles. Now, in her current predicament, she found herself resorting to marijuana and alcohol as coping mechanisms, choices that had led to her screwing her neighbor like they were sex-crazed teenagers having sex for the first time.

Those moments with Terry were thrilling, yet now filled her with conflict. She questioned what her life might become if this unplanned journey led her to 'Team Terry.' As Katie rambled to herself incoherently, her phone buzzed insistently in her apron pocket, likely a message from Terry. She clenched her fist but ignored the persistent vibrations, opting to turn to her canvas instead, seeking a distraction in her art.

With no clear vision, she painted vigorously, her strokes fueled by a mix of frustration and anxiety, humming to herself in an attempt to calm her mind. Seeking some semblance of peace, she closed her eyes and recalled her mother's words about finding inner tranquility amidst chaos or some other Kumbaya nonsense. Taking a deep breath, she looked up and half-jokingly, half-seriously said to the ceiling, "Okay, God, if you're up there, whatever you're doing, please don't choose today to teach me a lesson."

***

Terry repeatedly checked his phone, his brow furrowed in confusion. "Why isn't she responding?" he wondered aloud. Despite several calls and texts, Katie's silence was deafening. 'Today of all days,' Terry thought, frustrated that Katie had chosen this moment to shut down. Engrossed in his worry, Terry didn't notice Emily entering the kitchen.

With a look of concern, Emily approached him. "You okay, babe?" she inquired. Terry, preoccupied with his phone, hardly acknowledged her. Emily's gentle touch on his shoulder finally broke his trance. "Terry," she said softly, "What's wrong? You've been elsewhere lately, and I can't help but notice. You've been so distant. Is something up at work? You're always on your phone, and it's like you're here, but not really. Honestly, you look like you've lost your best friend, but since I'm right here, you're starting to scare me, big guy."

Terry turned to face Emily, offering a quick kiss. "I'm fine, Emmi bear. Work's just been hectic, but it'll settle down after today." His reassurance, however, didn't quite ring true. Emily, familiar with his tells, sensed something was off. The nickname "Emmi bear" hasn't carried the whole truth lately. Emily had started noticing subtle changes in Terry's behavior, like his increased secrecy about work and a constant attachment to his phone.

Emily tried to hide her frustration. "Well, make sure you take care of yourself. You're looking run down like you're getting sick with the flu or something," she said, concern lacing her voice. Terry forced a chuckle, flashed his best Hollywood smile, bid his farewells, and left for work, his mind still preoccupied with Katie's silence.

***

Alone in her car, Katie stared at the ultrasound in disbelief. "Oh my god, I'm actually pregnant," she whispered, the words feeling surreal. The words seemed unfamiliar, a surprising reality after all this time. While the news brought joy, there was a subtle sadness in realizing that this miracle disproved her being the cause of infertility. It also meant her future child would have to check "biracial" on their paperwork.

Her thoughts turned to James, her supportive and loving husband. A pang of despair gripped her heart as she considered the impact this would have on him. He didn't deserve this. He had been her rock, always there for her, even though sometimes she secretly wished he was more assertive. Pushing aside her guilt, she remembered her promise to meet Terry at their favorite spot – a restaurant they'd discovered during one of their rendezvous. She texted Terry she was on her way and began the 45-minute drive.

At the restaurant, Terry's astonishment mirrored her own. "You're really pregnant!" he exclaimed.

Katie, a mix of laughter and tears, said, "I know, right? How could something so tiny and in black and white be so beautiful?"

Terry stared in amazement, expressing his awe.

"It's yours," she confessed softly, taking his hand. Terry's eyes filled with tears. "I knew it," he whispered.

Confused, Katie asked, "What do you mean?"

Terry handed her a napkin, looked into her eyes, and explained, "I knew when we first found out. I just felt it – something changed that night."

Katie lightened the mood, "I definitely think it was that kinky potion that did this, not fate."

The remainder of their lunch was a blend of planning and laughter as they discussed future plans and guessed about their baby's features. For this moment, they found joy in their creation, momentarily forgetting about the impending drama and pain. Leaving the restaurant, Terry, with a broad smile, walked behind Katie, his arms around her waist, reveling in their happiness.

Terry escorted Katie to her car, where he grabbed her and kissed her passionately before kneeling and whispering to her belly, "Daddy loves you already," as he kissed Katie's stomach.

Amused, Katie giggled, "Would you stop? I gotta go." She kissed Terry on the cheek, got into her car, and drove away.

Only when Katie's car disappeared from view did Terry become aware of a figure across the parking lot. There stood Emily, her body rigid, eyes locked on the spot where he had just kissed Katie. Disbelief and pain etched across her face; she struggled to process the scene, her mouth open in shock, tears brimming in her eyes. Emily's heart sank with regret as she recalled activating the location sharing on Terry's phone, a decision that now unveiled a harsh truth.

In her mind, denial battled with reality. "This can't be happening. Terry wouldn't... not with someone else," she thought, her heart refusing to accept the scene before her.

Terry's gaze met Emily's. Realizing the magnitude of what she had seen, he rushed towards her, desperation in his voice. "Em, oh my god, baby, no, no, no," he said, his arms enveloping her in a futile attempt to comfort. Emily stood motionless, engulfed in a wave of astonishment and betrayal...

Love and a Colt .45

Samantha

Chapter Eighteen

There's a unique thrill in starting a new job and instantly clicking with someone who becomes your work best friend. That's precisely what happened on my first day at Thomason Surgical. Assigned as a surgical services rep in the Houston Medical Center, I was introduced to Samantha, my trainer, for the next three months. Samantha was a whirlwind of quirkiness and sass, quick to throw a side-eye or call out nonsense, and I absolutely loved it. Work suddenly transformed into days filled with laughter and learning, a stark contrast to my last job, which ended in a scandalous fiasco involving my boss and then-boyfriend – but that's a whole other can of worms to unpack.

Come Friday, after a week of productive bonding, Samantha and I decided to celebrate with a happy hour session at El Tiempo. Over our first round of margaritas, we dove deep into the stories of our lives. Samantha recounted her move from Chicago to Houston, a fresh start after a tumultuous divorce and a disastrous relationship. "Girl, Houston men are a different breed!" she exclaimed. I couldn't help but laugh. "Dating here is definitely an acquired taste," I agreed.

Samantha lamented her recent string of bad dates. "Just when I think it can't get worse, the next guy comes along as if to say, 'Hold my beer'."

"Not the 'hold my beer,'" I chuckled, nearly spitting out my drink.

As the conversation turned to me, I shared about my own divorce a few years ago and my six-year-old daughter. "Dating hasn't exactly been a priority," I admitted.

"Why not? You're stunning!" Samantha was genuinely perplexed.

I shrugged off her compliment. "I'm just not interested in settling for less."

"So, what, you're planning to become a nun?" she teased.

I laughed. "No, just holding out for something better."

Intrigued, Samantha leaned in. "Okay, spill it. What really happened in your marriage?"

"You first," I challenged.

"He was a serial cheater," she said indifferently, then quickly turned the focus back on me. "Your turn. What's your story?"

I hesitated, then admitted, "I think he loved the idea of me more than he actually loved me."

"And what made you leave Chicago and your family?" I prodded, sensing there was more to her story.

Realizing we were both harboring deep secrets, Samantha proposed a pact. "Let's lay it all out, no holding back, and then we never speak of it again."

"Damn, is it that serious?" I joked.

"You tell me," she said, her tone challenging.

"Alright, let's Fight Club this shit," I declared, downing my margarita.

Samantha smiled, then asked, "Who's going first?"

"I will," I said, taking a deep breath. "I slept with my husband's best friend."

Her eyes widened in shock. "Okay, that's...not what I was expecting."

Clearly nervous but committed to our pact, Samantha took another sip of her drink. "No judgment," she started, then dropped a bombshell. "I shot my ex-boyfriend."

I felt the color drain from my face, my hand shooting up to flag down the waiter. "We're going to need another round of margaritas. And keep them coming," I stammered.

"Yes, ma'am," the waiter replied, sensing the heavy atmosphere.

Samantha cleared her throat. "Let me explain," she began.

"I know," she said. "It sounds awful, but I had no choice." It was an obviously painful memory, as tears welled up in Samantha's eyes.

"I don't doubt that you did," I said as I reach out a hand to Samantha.

"That asshole is alive and fine somewhere, probably taking some other poor girl through hell just like he did to me and his ex before me," she said.

"Well, that's good he's alive; not good that he could be taking another woman through the wringer. What exactly happened to get to that point?"

"What didn't happen?!" Samantha said. As the waiter set down another round of margaritas, fresh chips, and salsa, Samantha took a sip and dived in head first.

It had to be about three months after my divorce, and I had just started working in the OR at Mount Sinai when I met this handsome and charismatic physician's assistant named Chase. I don't know if I was horny, love deprived, stupid, or all three, but he was everything I thought I was looking for in a man.

He was tall, with handsome, chocolate skin, kind brown eyes, and a smile that would melt the room and your vagina. His voice was deep and commanding. He had this attitude about him that exuded masculinity, like he knew exactly what to do. There was something about seeing him in those dark blue scrubs that would just set me off. It was clear he worked out in his off time, and he didn't miss a single spot. It seemed as if every part of his body had been chiseled to perfection.

I found myself unable to speak in this man's presence, and I felt he could sense that. Whenever I worked cases with him, he would do things like brush my neck or stand too close behind me when he tied my gown up. There was this electric intensity between us that was undeniable.

As I listened I couldn't help but blurt out, "Well, damn, I've never had anything like that while working in the OR."

"Yeah, well, it's probably for the best," Samantha said while eating a chip.

"Okay, so you guys are hot and heavy, so to speak," I said, prompting Samantha to continue.

Yes, something like that. Despite the intense attraction, there was so much more to it. We had so much in common. We liked the same shows, music, and food. He would stay after cases and help me turn over the room, and we would talk and laugh. It just felt so easy with him—nothing like when I was married to my husband, Jared.

Yes, we were attracted to each other and had things in common, but we drifted apart after we had the boys. Things that we used to do, like date nights, cooking together, hell, even just watching shows together, were replaced by late working nights and brief update conversations in passing. The only time we were in one place together was when it was time to go to bed. Even then, some nights, that wasn't the case. By the time I tried to correct our course, it was too late. Jared had been sleeping with half the neighborhood and then some. The crazy part was I wasn't even mad. I was just ready to get the boys and move on with my life.

In comparison, Chase was a welcomed change. Two months into our flirtation, we finally decided to exchange numbers.

Shocked, I interjected, "TWO MONTHS!"

Samantha chuckled before she responded saying, "I was struggling with the idea of talking to Chase. With all of his charm and looks, something in me just felt he was too good to be true, you know."

"I can definitely understand that. You move differently after divorce. You tell yourself that you are okay and ready to get back out there, but subconsciously, you are way more fucked up than you thought. It is a healing process on an emotional, mental, and physical level, so I get your hesitation," I said.

"Exactly!" Samantha says, nodding. Mulling over what I just said as if I had nailed everything she was feeling at that point in her life, Samantha started again.

We started texting immediately that afternoon. The conversation went from pleasantries and getting to know each other, to I can't wait to taste all of you and bend you over my couch.

"Well, that escalated quickly," I said teasingly.

Samantha shot me a look before laughing and saying, "Girl, I never stood a chance."

After all that texting about what we wanted to do to each other, I inevitably found myself at his apartment the next evening. The boys were with their father, granting me an evening of unbridled freedom. I didn't realize what I had been missing sexually, or maybe Jared and I had fallen into a lazy sexual pattern, but Chase knew exactly what he was doing that night. I arrived at his apartment Downtown around 9 PM; I had no clue what to expect.

I was nervous as all hell and, sensing my apprehension, Chase greeted me with a knowing smile and two glasses of wine. I gratefully accepted the glass. I downed the wine before even reaching the couch. His laughter filled the room as he gently took the empty glass from my hand, setting it aside on the coffee table.

It took what seemed like an eternity to meet his gaze, but when I finally did, the hunger in his eyes was unmistakable, a clear reflection of the desire burning within me. He gently traced his thumb across my bottom lip, sending shivers down my spine. His touch was electric, igniting a dormant fire extinguished within me long ago. When Chase's lips finally met mine, the world around us seemed to melt away. I could taste the lingering sweetness of the wine on his lips, its fruity notes mingling with the intensity of our kiss.

He pulled me onto his lap, and I felt his hands move up my thighs and under my dress. I could feel him squeeze my ass as he pulled me closer to him. Our kisses became more vigorous as our desire for one another overpowered our judgment.

I didn't even seem to care when he ripped the front of my dress open to expose my breasts. His caresses were both gentle and demanding before pulling aside the sheer fabric of my bra to reveal my nipples. I couldn't help but moan as he gently bit and sucked each one.

My hands, almost of their own accord, reached for his massive cock that seemed to grow harder with each passing moment. As I began to undo the button on his pants, Chase lifted me effortlessly, carrying me to the bedroom with a strength that left me breathless. He laid me down as he pulled my panties off. I watched this gorgeous man before me undress, and I couldn't help but be astonished at the sheer length and girth of his cock before me. I was eager and scared, but my desire overruled my fear.

Before I could act on my impulses, he had taken my hands and pinned them above my head. His gaze locked onto mine as he slid two fingers into my wet pussy. I gasped as he moved his fingers within me in a rhythmic motion. My eyes closed, and I became lost in the pleasure; I could feel myself nearing that inevitable moment of pure ecstasy.

I felt the heat emanating from Chase as he whispered in my ear, "You are so fucking wet, and it's turning me on to know I do this to you." As he kissed my neck, the wave of my orgasm washed over me, causing me to cry out as the sheer intensity of it all was overwhelming. As I laid there, reason returned to my body, and the haze of orgasmic bliss departed; I knew at that moment that I was undoubtedly fucked.

Chapter Nineteen

As I reclined in the booth, a mix of margaritas, spicy salsa, and Samantha's steamy story set my senses ablaze.

"Wow, I'm speechless," as I tried to regain my composure. "Girl, I can see why you felt that way."

Samantha chuckled, her eyes twinkling with the memories. "Right?!"

She leaned in, her voice dropping to a conspiratorial tone.

"So there I was, six months in, living out every sexual fantasy I could ever think of. It was all so addictive. Before I knew it, he'd met my boys, we'd moved in together, and everything just clicked. I had ultimately let my guard down, and I was undoubtedly head over heels in love with this man. I should have known that the other shoe would eventually drop, but I was happy until it did.

Work was great, and the boys adored him. They would spend their afternoons after school doing homework and their evenings playing video games together. On the weekends, when they would go to their father's house, our time together would be an endless adventure through Chicago, while dessert at home would be exploring each other's bodies. What more could a woman ask for?

As we moved into a new year, that's when the other shoe started to wiggle. We were at dinner on a Saturday when Chase started mentioning marriage and expanding our family. He had no children of his own, even though he treated mine as his.

Samantha took a thoughtful sip of her margarita, her eyes reflecting a mix of nostalgia and pain.

I had to tell Chase the hard truth: I couldn't have more children. My body had been through a lot during my second pregnancy, leading my doctor to recommend a tubal ligation. It was a tough decision, but necessary for my health. I could see the disappointment in his eyes at the realization that expanding our family was not an option. I added insult to injury while sharing my feelings on marriage. I was open to the idea of marrying again, but after my divorce, I was hesitant to rush into anything. I suggested we should enjoy our time together and revisit the idea later. That conversation didn't sit well with him either.

"Ouch! That sounds like a delicate situation," I commented, imagining the strain it must have put on their relationship.

"Exactly," Samantha continued.

February became a relentless campaign of 'wooing Samantha, with Chase pulling out all the stops. Chase was determined to change my mind about marriage, IVF, and surrogacy, believing they were what our family needed. But the more he pushed, the more I pulled away. His persistence, rather than drawing me in, started to push me further away. I couldn't pinpoint why, but something inside me was resisting.

By March, I had reached my breaking point. I had to be honest with him – and with myself. I admitted I didn't want any more children and that it was okay if he needed to find someone who shared his desire for a family. Chase insisted he was okay with just having me, but I could sense a shift in him. It was subtle at first, but there was a change in the way he looked at me, in his touch. That's when I knew it was the beginning of the end for us.

"Was there something about him that made you not want to have more children?" I asked, intrigued.

Samantha paused, considering the question before answering. "Honestly, it wasn't anything he did. On some level, I knew something so good would never last, and when I looked at him, I could not envision bringing a child into that kind of uncertainty. I think he could sense that, too."

"That makes sense," I said, understanding her dilemma.

Samantha continued, her voice growing somber.

By May, Chase was a stranger to me. I saw a completely different side of him. We fought constantly. He grew distant from the boys. Our once adventurous Chicago weekends were now spent with me in the bedroom watching TV and him in the living room playing video games.

I knew things were over in June when I came back home after being on call at the hospital late one Sunday night. He didn't hear me come into the house, but I could hear him on the phone with his mom.

His words were like daggers.

"I just don't get her. Any woman would be dying to get married and have a family, but not her. I'm here fucking begging her, and she refuses, but she expects me to play dad to her fucking kids but won't give me my own. It's bullshit!" Chase said, annoyed.

I gasped, feeling the sting of his words.

"Well, sweetie, maybe she isn't the one for you. I completely agree that it is unfair that you have to be a father to her kids but won't even consider having a family with you. She's a selfish bitch. You deserve better, and you are right. You are a catch, and any woman would be lucky to marry you and have your children," his mom, said defiantly.

I stood unable to move, shocked at the audacity of them both. His following words were a complete gut punch.

"If she thinks it is okay to lay around and have children by another man and I play daddy to them, then she has another thing coming. Fuck her and those kids." Chase said bitterly.

I turned and walked back out of the house as his mom made murmurings of approval. I didn't even care if he heard me as the door slammed behind me. I got back in my car and drove off. His name flashed across my phone repeatedly as call after call came through. The other shoe had finally dropped.

Chapter Twenty

Samantha's tale left me speechless, her account so raw and vivid it was almost tangible. Her poise belied the turmoil beneath, the memories still vivid and searing. I could hardly fathom the strength it took to not lash out in the face of such betrayal.

Shaking off my own incredulity, I found my voice. "I can't even begin to understand the pain you must have felt then," I said.

Samantha gave a wry smile, her eyes distant. "It was surreal, really. I felt an almost paralyzing numbness."

I hesitated, unable to hold back. "What happened next? I'm almost afraid to ask."

Samantha took a deep breath, another sip of her margarita fortifying her. "Well, you would be right to. It definitely wasn't pretty."

She dove back into her narrative.

It was the lead-up to July 4th, three weeks since that fateful night I overheard Chase. His calls were constant, but I couldn't face him, not yet. I managed to sneak back to our place for a few essentials for the boys and me. We holed up in a hotel, trying to make sense of it all. I knew it was over, but I wasn't ready for the final showdown.

The day before July 4th, Chase called again. I finally picked up. His apologies poured through the phone, desperate and rehearsed. He claimed he didn't mean any of it; he was just angry and venting. But his words rang hollow, his once cherished voice now grating to my ears. I never understood the saying there's a thin line between love and hate until that very moment. He suggested dinner on July 4th at my favorite restaurant. The very idea made my skin crawl, but I agreed. The boys were with their dad, and I needed closure; plus, I had to retrieve the rest of our belongings.

As I entered the restaurant, there he was, looking as charming as ever. But the sight of him only stirred anger within me. He tried to approach me cautiously, but I could barely conceal my disdain. The evening was a rollercoaster of emotions. At moments, the anger gave way to nostalgia, a reminder of the man I once fell for. His wit, charm, and the memories of our better days momentarily softened my resolve.

For a fleeting second, I wondered if his harsh words were just a product of his frustration over our dashed dreams. In the pain of that realization, I found a sliver of understanding. Despite his cold words cutting through me like a knife that night, for the first time since everything fell apart, I found myself questioning if there might still be a spark, a glimmer of what we once had.

"Samantha, are you serious right now?" I asked, my voice laced with bewilderment.

Samantha exhaled deeply, her face clouded with a mix of regret and self-reproach. "I know, it sounds crazy," she admitted, her voice tinged with a hint of shame. "In that moment, I just got swept up.

He was there, pouring out apologies and sharing his feelings, and for a brief instant, I found myself empathizing with him. But looking back, I was a fucking idiot."

I nodded, biting back my initial reaction to keep the conversation open and supportive. Samantha sighed, the weight of her past decisions evident in her demeanor as she continued her story.

The night had been unfolding beautifully when, after a delightful dinner, Chase suggested we check out a new jazz club nearby. In hindsight, I should have known better and taken my ass home. But the evening's charm lured me in, and I found myself agreeing.

Inside the club, the atmosphere was intoxicating — smooth jazz, dim lighting, and the clink of glasses set the perfect scene. We found ourselves lost in the rhythm, dancing and laughing, rekindling the spark that had brought us together. It felt like old times, and everything seemed right again for a moment.

Post-dance, Chase excused himself to the restroom, and I headed to the bar to replenish our drinks. That's when a familiar face from the OR greeted me. Patrick, a resident I frequently collaborated with on surgical cases, stood before me. In the sterile environment of the OR, personal identities often blur, masked by the uniformity of scrubs and surgical attire. Yet, there was something unmistakable about Patrick – it was his eyes. Even during complex procedures, his eyes always conveyed a sense of calm and kindness, a soothing presence amidst the intensity of surgery. That familiar, reassuring gaze was what gave him away in this unexpected encounter outside the confines of the hospital.

He stood a striking figure with a lean, muscular build that spoke of quiet strength. His hair was immaculately styled, complementing the well-groomed beard that framed his chiseled features. But the subtle scent of his cologne truly captivated me, a rich and alluring aroma that made my knees tremble with an unexpected weakness. His presence was unexpectedly charming, and I found myself stunned by how different he looked outside of work. We chatted amiably as he insisted on buying us drinks — a friendly gesture that I couldn't decline.

However, unbeknownst to me, Chase was observing us the whole time, a storm brewing within him. As I turned to rejoin Chase with drinks in hand, I watched, perplexed, as he stormed out of the club. Confused, I followed him, leaving Patrick to watch our table.

Outside, Chase was pacing, his demeanor a mix of anger and betrayal. "What's wrong?" I asked, genuinely baffled.

His response blindsided me. "So, this is what we're doing now? Flirting with some white guy while I'm away? You just had to ruin the evening." His accusations were absurd.

I tried to explain, "That's just Patrick, a colleague. You're overreacting." But my attempts to calm him only fueled his rage. He hurled insults, accusing me of disrespect and unfaithfulness.

"I don't give a fuck who it is; you are disrespectful as fuck like always," he snips.

Frustrated and exhausted by the unfounded accusations, I declared the night over and returned to the club. Patrick, concerned, offered to escort me to my car, but I refused, wanting only to leave the night's drama behind.

But as I reached my car, Chase was there, waiting. He pleaded for a chance to talk, and against my better judgment, I agreed.

As I sat down in the driver's seat, the unthinkable happened. Chase's hands were suddenly around my throat, squeezing with a ferocity that left me gasping for air. In a desperate struggle, I fought back, but he was relentless, his grip tightening. With terrifying ease, he hoisted me up and hurled me across the car, my body crashing between the driver and passenger seats into the back seat. The impact was brutal; my head collided with a back seat belt buckle, sending a searing jolt of pain through my skull.

He relentlessly continued his assault, bashing my head against the seat as his hands constricted around my neck. I fought back desperately, scratching, hitting, and kicking in a frantic bid for survival, but he seemed unfazed. His voice, filled with rage and accusation, pierced through the chaos: "You made me do this!" His words echoed in the confined space, amplifying the horror of the moment.

As the darkness began to encroach on the edges of my vision, I could feel the grasp of life slipping away. In those harrowing moments, a flash of realization hit me — my .45, which I'd absentmindedly left in the back seat pocket after a visit to the shooting range. Usually, it never would have been there, but fate had intervened in my favor.

With fading strength, I reached desperately for the pocket and grasped the gun. If Chase had been less consumed by his violent rage, he might have noticed the distinct sound of the gun being cocked. But he didn't, and that was his mistake. I pulled the trigger without aiming, driven by a pure instinct for survival. The gunshot exploded in the confined space, a deafening roar that was swiftly followed by his screams: "You shot me!"

Suddenly, his choking grasp released me, and air flooded back into my lungs. I struggled to gather my senses, no longer pinned under his assault and my head being used as a whack-a-mole mallet. With great effort, I dragged myself fully into the back seat and stumbled out of the car, the gun still clutched in my trembling hand.

Chase's cries still echoed behind me — "You fucking shot me" — a mantra of his disbelief and pain. Dizzy and disoriented, I managed only a few steps before my legs gave out, and I collapsed onto the cold ground.

In that moment of darkness closing in, I heard a voice call out, and then a figure loomed over me, lifting me up. As consciousness slipped away, the last thing I saw was the blur of a face, and everything faded to black.

"Samantha," I exclaimed, my voice a mixture of shock and compassion. "I'm so incredibly sorry you had to go through that."

Samantha waved off my sympathy with a slight smile. "You don't need to apologize. It was a horrendous experience, but it's behind me now. In a twisted way, it taught me a lesson I'll never forget."

I hesitated, unsure how to continue, but curiosity got the better of me. "What happened after you lost consciousness? Who was there for you?"
"Oh, right," Samantha said, realizing she had left a tantalizing thread hanging.

Later, I woke up in the hospital, and there was Patrick right by my side. In the chaos, I had left my phone behind in the club, and he'd followed me to return it. He witnessed the shooting and immediately called for help. He told the police it was self-defense, which I confirmed. Thankfully, the law was on my side, especially when they discovered Chase's violent past with his ex-girlfriend. He brutally attacked her, causing her to miscarry. It was a shocking revelation; I never knew that side of him. I consider myself fortunate that I escaped a potentially worse fate.

I was stunned. "That's horrific, especially what he did to his ex-girlfriend. It's unsettling to think how little we can know about someone."

"Yeah, she was expecting twins. He could have had a family, but his jealousy and rage destroyed everything." Samantha's voice trailed off, her eyes clouding with the memory.

Changing the subject, I asked, "So, what about Patrick?"

A blush crept onto Samantha's cheeks, and she smiled sheepishly. "Why do you assume something happened with Patrick?"

I laughed. "That blush and your smile are more telling than you think."

Samantha playfully dodged the question. "Patrick's story is for another time, perhaps over another round of happy hour drinks."

"Oh, you can't leave me hanging like that!" I protested, eager to hear more.

Samantha raised her glass, her eyes twinkling. "Alright, enough about me. It's your turn now. Tell me about what happened with your husband's best friend." She settled back, ready for my tale.

Anchored Affair

Kimber

Chapter Twenty-One

As Samantha sat across from me, her eyes wide with anticipation, I knew it was my turn to unravel the secrets of my past. The memories cascaded through my mind, a montage of sweet and bitter moments.

"Well, my story might not hold a candle to yours," I began with a nervous laugh, taking a sip of my margarita for courage.

Samantha leaned in, her curiosity piqued. "Why the hesitation?" she inquired.

"I was young, maybe a bit naive," I confessed, recalling those days with fondness and regret.

"Go on," she encouraged, her hand motioning for me to continue.

My story begins in my first year of college. It was in a biology class that I first saw Jackson. I always sat at the front — partly to be a diligent student, but mostly because it gave me a perfect view to people-watch. Jackson was impossible to miss. He was tall, with fair skin from his Irish heritage, neatly cut blonde hair, piercing green eyes that seemed to see right through you, and a body sculpted with muscles. The complete bad boy accessory pack with matching tattoos. He was six years my senior, an enigma wrapped in a mystery and utterly captivating.

Samantha listened, her expression a mix of amusement and intrigue.

He had this aura of a bad boy that every girl in class seemed to notice but couldn't quite capture his attention. Week after week, I watched as numerous attempts to flirt with him were met with utter disinterest. I don't know what came over me, but I remember walking up to him at the end of one class, introducing myself, and boldly telling him he was having lunch with me on Wednesday. Before he could even respond, I walked away, leaving him dazed and confused. Surprisingly, he showed up for lunch, calling me 'crazy' in the most endearing way, and from that moment, we were inseparable.

I paused, reminiscing about those early days.

Jackson was my first real relationship, my first everything, and at nineteen, I fell hard. He was tough to read, a true Marine, always composed and a bit mysterious. We had a whirlwind first year — traveling around the state, salsa dancing on date nights, or just lounging around playing video games surrounded by snacks. During that year, Jackson lived with his childhood best friend, Hayden.

Hayden was his complete opposite — average height, dark curly hair tailored to his face, deep brown eyes, and an infectious smile paired with a razor-sharp wit.

Nothing particularly stood out about him, but there was an air to him that made him irresistible, maybe even more so than Jackson. Yet, Hayden hadn't exactly been my most ardent supporter. He viewed me as too young and more trouble than I was worth.

Each time I visited Jackson's place, I silently wished Hayden wouldn't be around. His presence stirred a peculiar kind of tension within me, a blend of awkwardness and an inexplicable pull, perhaps an underlying attraction I couldn't fully understand or articulate. His presence was unsettling to my spirit. So, you can imagine my relief when Jackson and I moved in together after that first year.

Life seemed to fall into place after that. I continued my psychology major, and Jackson transitioned into firefighting. When we got engaged in our second year, it felt like everything was as it should be.

Samantha's eyes sparkled with curiosity. "I have to know, what was your engagement like? I'm a sucker for a good proposal story," she said, her smile wide with expectation.

I hesitated, the memory bittersweet. "Well, it was... unconventional," I began. "Jackson simply bought a ring and asked if I wanted it. There was no romantic proposal, no getting down on one knee. Just the ring and a question."

Samantha blinked, taken aback. "He just... handed you the ring?"

"Yes, exactly as I said. No fanfare, no grand gesture. Accepting the ring was the unspoken agreement that we were engaged," I explained, feeling the disappointment anew.

Samantha's smile faded, replaced by a sympathetic frown. "I'm so sorry. That's not the dream proposal anyone imagines."

I nodded, my own disillusionment echoing in her reaction. "It was utterly underwhelming. I had fantasized about a magical proposal since I was a little girl, and what I got was nothing like I had hoped. It was a secret disappointment I couldn't even voice."

Samantha quickly apologized, realizing her reaction might have been hurtful. "I didn't mean to make you feel bad. It's just not the typical story you hear."

"I know," I replied, a bit tersely. "But that was just the beginning."

I had always dreamt of a lavish wedding, surrounded by friends and family. Instead, our 'big day' was reduced to a brief, ten-minute ceremony at city hall, with just our parents in attendance. Sure, I had Jackson, the man every girl envied me for, but it felt like something crucial was missing.

After the wedding, Jackson joined the city fire department and threw himself into work. I was proud of him, but his dedication meant he was hardly ever home. When he was, he was too exhausted to do anything but sleep. Honestly, after we got married, it felt like Jackson's efforts just faded away. It was as if he had already 'won' the prize in his mind — he got the girl, and that was it. To him, I was like a trophy, something to be admired occasionally, placed on a shelf and only given attention sporadically when he happened to remember. I began to feel more and more isolated.

Then, the unthinkable occurred - my grandfather passed suddenly from a stroke. For me, his passing was especially shattering. My grandfather had been a rock in my life, a steady presence I always relied on. Countless days of my childhood were spent by his side, exploring new places, tending to the garden, cooking together, and sharing laughter over our favorite TV shows. His passing felt like losing a part of my soul.

In such times of deep sorrow, one naturally seeks comfort in one's partner. But when I turned to Jackson, hoping for solace, I was met with cold indifference. His response to my grief was a blunt reminder that death is an inevitable part of life, followed by words that are etched painfully in my memory: "At least he didn't suffer." The insensitivity of that remark ignited a fury in me. I yearned for his support and empathy, but he was emotionally unavailable, retreating further into his work as if to escape the situation, to escape me.

Feeling alone, I shut down and drifted through the days like a mere ghost. I was physically present but emotionally absent, a shell moving through life's motions without truly living. In an attempt to process my grief and find some semblance of peace, I decided to take a break from school for the summer. I needed that time to mourn, reflect, and gather the scattered pieces of my heart.

During this period of solitude, my emotions transformed. I began to harbor a deep-seated resentment and anger towards Jackson. His absence in my time of dire need, his lack of compassion, and his inability to understand my pain weighed heavily on me. It was a loneliness that seeped into the very marrow of my being.

By the time fall arrived, I was ready to return to my studies, to find some trace of normalcy again. But life had yet another twist in store for me: I was pregnant."

Samantha's reaction was a mix of shock and disbelief. "Seriously?!" she gasped. "But how? I mean, I understand the mechanics, but how?"

Laughing, I replied, "I've asked myself the same thing. I remember thinking, 'When did Jackson and I even last have sex?'"

Our laughter echoed in the room, a brief lull from the gravity of the situation.

Reflecting on that particular night, I admitted, "Looking back, the sex was unremarkable. It was more about me seeking a connection, anything to pull me out of the overwhelming grief. It was like clinging to a life preserver amid an emotional storm."

Samantha's expression was a blend of empathy and sadness. "Kimber, that's genuinely heartbreaking. Love shouldn't feel so empty, you know? Despite the chaos in my marriage, I had some passionate moments at least. The sex was good, and strangely, he was dependable. Sure, he slept with half the town, but when it really mattered, when his family needed him, he was present and accounted for."

"I know," I sighed, the memories flooding back. "I missed all the warning signs.

My doctor had switched my birth control due to daily migraines, and suddenly, I was eating non-stop and constantly running to the bathroom. I foolishly blamed the new medication. It wasn't until the night of my best friend's bachelorette party that the truth hit me.

Everyone was pre-gaming and egging me on to take shots before the limo arrived, but I felt off. They joked about me being pregnant, so to shut them down, I took a pregnancy test. To everyone's shock, including mine, it read 'Pregnant.' At first, I thought it was a prank because Alicia pulled the test out of her bag way too fast, but after two more positive tests, reality sank in."

"Damn," Samantha murmured, clearly stunned.

"Yeah," I chuckled ruefully. "Not exactly the best way to find out, especially right before a bachelorette party. In hindsight, I might have taken it as a sign to take my ass home."

Curious, Samantha asked, "Why do you say that?"

"Because," I began, a nostalgic look in my eyes

At the very first bar of our supposed epic bar crawl, I ran into Hayden. I never felt more alive than the moment our eyes met from across the bar. I didn't know what it was, but I had to have him. It was a feeling I hadn't experienced in so long.

Chapter Twenty-Two

Samantha looked at me intently, her eyes sparkling with inquisitive suspicion. "Do you think running into Hayden was just a coincidence, or could it have been something more? Are you active on social media?" she probed.

I nodded, "I do have social media accounts, but honestly, I'm not very active. I mainly use them to watch videos. I'd like to believe our meeting was just a stroke of fate."

"How long had it been since you last saw him?" Samantha's interest was piqued.

"Nearly three years," I responded a hint of sentimentality in my voice.

Leaning back, Samantha's face lit up with anticipation. "Your story is holding its own," she chuckled. "Go on."

I resumed, recalling the moment vividly.

As our eyes met across the crowded bar, it was as if we were magnets being pulled together. Suddenly, he was right there before me. My heart skipped a beat as he greeted me and wrapped me in a heartfelt hug. His rich and earthy scent of cologne tantalized my senses, evoking a spark deep in my core. Time seemed to stand still in his embrace. It was only when Marie approached, interrupting the moment with a casual 'hey,' that I was jolted back to reality.

"Hey, what's up?" I responded, slightly disoriented.

"We're heading to the next bar. You coming?" Marie asked, her gaze shifting between Hayden and me, sensing a trace of something unspoken.

"Yeah, let's go," I replied, tearing myself away to follow her.

As we navigated through the crowd, I couldn't resist casting one last glance at Hayden. Our eyes locked, and in that fleeting moment, I saw my turmoil reflected in his gaze. Back in the limo, my phone vibrated with a message from an unknown number. The message was simple yet loaded with implication: "Dinner?" My heart raced as I realized who it must be from. I stared at the screen, torn. Eventually, I decided it was best not to follow the white rabbit down the hole. I tucked my phone away, focusing on enjoying the rest of the night.

The following day, lost in thought over my coffee, Jackson's entrance startled me. I was so deep in reflection I hardly noticed him until he tapped my shoulder.

"Jumpy much?" he remarked, surprised by my reaction. "Did you even hear what I said?"

"What?" I replied, snapping back to the present, noticing his growing irritation.

"I talked to Hayden last night. We're having dinner with him in two weeks, on Thursday."

The coffee I was sipping spewed from my mouth in shock. "What is wrong with you?" Jackson was visibly annoyed.

"I, um, I'm pregnant," I blurted out, the words tumbling out in a rush.

Jackson's complexion turned a pale white, his fair skin losing all its color as shock drained the blood from his face. "How the hell did this happen? Aren't you on birth control?" he stammered, astonishment etched in his features.

His reaction caught me off guard, and I retorted defensively, "Yes, I am. But you know, sometimes shit happens!"

He frowned, visibly unsettled. "This isn't part of our plan," he asserted.

"Our plan? It seems more like it's just you living your life while I'm left to fend for myself," I countered, frustration creeping into my voice.

He sighed heavily, attempting a more reasoned approach. "Look, Kimber, I don't think I'm ready for kids. My career is really taking off, and a promotion is on the horizon. A child could complicate things."

I shot back, equally adamant, "Well, it's a bit late for second thoughts now, isn't it? I'm on the verge of graduating, with plans for a Master's degree. I wasn't planning on a baby either."

He hesitated, then suggested, almost hesitantly, "You're not far along, right? Maybe there's still a way out...," his voice trailing off, implying an option too grave to articulate fully.

Fury and disbelief surged through me. "Are you fucking kidding me right now, Jackson?" I exploded, incredulous at his insensitivity.

"I'm just thinking of what's best for both of us," he defended, seemingly oblivious to the gravity of his words.

In a flash of anger, I hurled my coffee cup at him. It shattered against the wall, ceramic shards and coffee splattering everywhere.

"What the fuck, Kimber!" he shouted as I stormed out, slamming the bedroom door behind me, leaving him amidst the chaos of broken ceramic and spilled coffee.

***

The ensuing week passed in a haze. I broke the news of my pregnancy to my parents, and their excitement was overwhelming. It was a bittersweet moment for me, a stark reminder that this joyous occasion unfolded in a way I never imagined. I had never particularly yearned for children, but I always believed that if I did become pregnant, it would be a moment of shared happiness with my husband. Instead, I found myself facing the prospect of going through the pregnancy essentially alone. Jackson's presence had become even scarcer, his interactions with me limited to pressuring me about terminating the pregnancy.

Thankfully, I managed to secure an appointment with my OB the following Thursday. The doctor confirmed I was eight weeks along, and hearing my baby's heartbeat was transformative. In that instant, all of Jackson's demands faded away; I knew I wanted this child, and I was determined to make it work.

I received a text as I left the doctor's office, still elated from the appointment. It was from Hayden: "Auntie Pasta's 8 PM." The dinner plans had completely slipped my mind amidst the whirlwind of recent events. Glancing at the time, I realized I had just a few hours to get ready.

Arriving home, I quickly started preparing for the evening. Jackson walked in around 7 PM, and I casually said, "Hey, we need to leave soon for dinner with Hayden."

"What?" Jackson said with an attitude, dropping his gear on the floor and undressing.

"Dinner with Hayden tonight," I said, reminding him.

His response was curt and dismissive. "I'm not going," he stated flatly before heading to the shower.

Confused, I prodded, "But you set this up. Did you even tell Hayden you're not coming? You certainly didn't tell me!"

His reply was sharp and final. "I said I'm not going; just drop it," he snapped.

I stood there, contemplating my next move. Deciding not to engage in another argument, I continued getting ready.

Jackson, emerging from the shower, noticed me putting on my earrings. "What are you doing?" he asked, surprised.

"I'm going to dinner," I replied, slipping on my heels and grabbing my purse.

"Why bother?" he questioned, his tone a mix of confusion and frustration.

"Because I'd rather spend my evening enjoying a nice dinner than being stuck in this fucking apartment with you," I answered firmly, stepping out the door, leaving Jackson and our tensions behind.

Chapter Twenty-Three

As I arrived at the restaurant, my earlier confidence in confronting Jackson quickly dissolved into a bundle of nerves at the prospect of meeting Hayden. "What the fuck was I thinking?" I wondered aloud.

Samantha, snapping back to the present moment, caught the expression I was wearing and read it effortlessly. She playfully interjected, sipping her last margarita, "Exactly what I was wondering," signaling the waiter for another round.

Samantha leaned in, "From what you've shared, there seems to be some unresolved tension between you and Hayden. It's almost like he had feelings for you, but Jackson got to you first."

I nodded in agreement, acknowledging the accuracy of her observation. "You know, that's quite perceptive of you. That dinner turned out to be quite the eye-opener, revealing things in more ways than one."

Samantha's eyes twinkled with anticipation. "This is it. I know it."

Stepping into Auntie Pasta's, I paused at the entrance to scan the room for Hayden. My heart fluttered as I felt a familiar aura emanating from behind me.

"Hey, stranger," he said, his voice deep and alluring.

I turned, finding myself lost in the depths of his gaze as we embraced. His head lingered seductively near my neck, a subtle gesture as if to savor the essence of my being. A hidden hunger stirred within me, an unbidden desire for his lips to grace my skin. He appeared different, almost altered by time, or perhaps it was I who had changed, my senses clouded by the memories of Jackson. Our embrace seemed to last forever, a reluctance on both of our parts. I eventually stepped back, severing the intoxicating closeness that had enveloped us.

"Umm," I began, trying to regain my composure. "Shall we get a table?"

Hayden's gaze briefly swept the room. "Where's Jackson?" he inquired, his eyes darting to the parking lot.

"He's not coming," I replied, my voice flat at the thought of my earlier encounter with Jackson.

Hayden shook his head ruefully. "Why am I not surprised? I've been trying to catch up with him for months, but he's always too busy with work."

"That sounds about right," I agreed as we turned to the hostess.

Hayden's question caught me off guard. "I don't understand why you're here. You could've just canceled. Frankly, I was half-expecting him to bail anyway," he remarked.

I sighed, a hint of frustration present in my voice. "That's exactly why I decided to come. I'm tired of everything being on Jackson's terms. He never seems to consider anyone else's feelings or schedules for that matter..."

"Easy there, tiger," Hayden interjected, a hint of humor in his voice as he saw my rising annoyance. "Let's just sit down, relax, and have a drink."

He requested a table for two, his hand gently resting on the small of my back as we were led to our table by the hostess. Our waiter, Chris, arrived shortly and asked for our drink orders.

"Just water for me," I said quietly.

Hayden chuckled, "Just water? After the way you were going on a minute ago?"

I looked up from the menu and said, "I'm pregnant, so yes, water."

Hayden, visibly surprised, quickly recovered. "Water for me, too, then. Add a slice of lemon, please."

Chris nodded, his expression betraying a hint of curiosity about our conversation, but he moved on.

Hayden, with a knowing smirk, acknowledged the tension. "Seems like I've missed quite a bit," he said, gently taking the menu from my hands, which I hadn't realized I'd been clutching so tightly, and setting it on the table. "You know, you can talk to me. I may have given you the impression that I didn't care much for you, but that wasn't about you. I had my reasons."

I found myself opening up to Hayden, pouring out everything from our lackluster engagement and city hall wedding to the heartache of my grandfather's death and now the unexpected pregnancy. When I finally paused, a sense of relief washed over me, as if I had been carrying a burden I hadn't fully acknowledged.

Hayden reclined slightly, his fingers weaving thoughtfully through his short, curly locks. A moment of contemplation washed over his features as he absorbed the weight of my words. "Wow, that's... quite a lot," he said, the sincerity in his voice unmistakable. "I wish I had been aware of all this earlier. I would have stood by your side. But Jackson, well, he distanced himself, creating a rift between us. Don't misunderstand; we maintain contact, yet it's nothing like how we used to be." His eyes held a tinge of regret, reflecting a complex mix of emotions stirred by the untold stories and missed opportunities.

"Yeah," I replied, taking a sip of water. "I didn't mean to unload on you like that. I guess I've been bottling up my emotions all this time."

Hayden looked at me, his expression serious. "I have to say, and please don't take this the wrong way, but I never thought you and Jackson would last this long. Part of me almost hoped you wouldn't."

Confused by his admission, I could only muster a startled "What?" as a flurry of questions began swirling in my mind.

Hayden's insights struck a chord, shedding light on aspects of Jackson I hadn't fully acknowledged. "Jackson's always had this self-centered streak," he explained.

"We've known each other since childhood, and he's always been driven to be the best, no matter the cost. That's what led his ex-fiancé, Sarah, to cheat and leave. I'm not saying she was right, but Jackson's obsessive nature can be overpowering. When we were kids playing football, during his time in the Marines, and even now as a firefighter, he's always pushing to excel, often at the expense of others. This was my concern with your relationship. Once the initial excitement faded, I feared he might do the same to you. You're young, vibrant, and kind-hearted. I didn't want to see that light in you dimmed by him."

His words resonated deeply, echoing my own experiences with Jackson. "Too late," I said regretfully. "He's already done that."

Fighting back tears, I felt overwhelmed by the truth of the situation. "No, Kimber," Hayden interjected softly, trying to provide comfort. "I feel like a fucking idiot. I didn't mean to upset you."

"I know," I replied, dabbing at my eyes with a napkin.

"This isn't what I imagined marriage would be like. It's like living with a roommate who barely acknowledges me. He's either working non-stop, barely talking, or using me for sex on his terms. It's as if my own desires and needs don't matter. If I so much as suggest or attempt to try something new, then I'm accused of cheating or made to feel like I am being ridiculous. I get so sick of hearing 'you have a home, a car, and everything you could possibly need. What more do you want?!' A fucking husband! How about that?! And then the baby... it's like he doesn't even care. I might as well be a single mom."

As I broke down, feeling the full weight of my unhappiness, Hayden gently wiped away my tears. His gaze was intense and sincere. "He doesn't understand what he has in you. You're beautiful in every way. I'd be honored to have someone like you in my life, to have a family with you. If he can't see that, he's a fool. You deserve someone who truly sees and loves you. I wouldn't take a single moment for granted with you."

A heavy, charged silence hung between us, his words echoing in my mind. I was already questioning my marriage, and Hayden's frankness only intensified these doubts. I found myself at a loss for words, absorbing the gravity of his insight. Hayden had articulated thoughts and fears that had been silently gnawing at me, the same ones I had wrestled with in solitude since my grandfather's passing. I had yet to share these thoughts with my loved ones, a private turmoil I had endured alone.

As I stared into Hayden's eyes, I saw an unmistakable depth of earnestness and sincerity. His gaze held a genuine understanding and concern that spoke volumes, confirming the authenticity of his words. In that moment, surrounded by the quiet intensity of our exchange, I felt a connection with Hayden that transcended mere words.

Trying to lighten the mood, Hayden joked, "Man, this water is hitting hard tonight. Let's not talk about that asshole anymore. Tonight was supposed to be about me, remember?"

Curious, I managed to smile. "And how is that?"

His expression grew serious. "I've decided to re-enlist in the Navy. I'm leaving next week."

Shocked, I blurted out, "WHAT?!" drawing glances from nearby tables.

Seeing the emotion in my response, Hayden attempted to deflect with a hint of playful bravado. "Now, now, don't shed tears for this humble sailor," he said with a self-deprecating smile. "I'm about to embark on a grand voyage across the vast oceans in pursuit of untold adventures... it's not working, is it?"

"No," I replied unenthusiastically.

Hayden explained, "School just isn't working out, and I haven't been happy in any job since leaving the service. I need time to figure out what I want, so I'm returning to the Navy."

His news left me speechless, a mix of emotions churning within as I processed this unexpected turn of events. This evening might be the last time I see Hayden. Despite not being close, a sense of impending loss tugged at my heart, a poignant reminder of the unique bond we shared, however unspoken or undefined it was. Shaking off these gloomy thoughts, I decided to shift the mood of our evening.

With a newfound resolve, I offered a light-hearted suggestion, my smile returning. "Looks like we should make the most of your last days of freedom, huh?" I said, lifting my water glass in a toast. Hayden's face lit up with a warm, infectious smile as he clinked his glass against mine. "Absolutely," he agreed, his voice imbued with excitement and nostalgia, "Let's celebrate indeed."

The evening unfolded with an ease and laughter that belied our years apart. Surprisingly, our conversation flowed as if we were old friends reuniting, discovering shared interests and experiences that seemed endless. Before we knew it, time had slipped away, leaving us as the last patrons in the now quiet restaurant.

Glancing around at the vacant tables and chairs being stacked, I couldn't help but laugh awkwardly. "Looks like it's time to head out," I said, a hint of hesitancy in my voice. Hayden agreed, and we began to gather our belongings.

Outside, under the dim glow of the streetlights, a moment of uncertainty gripped me as we reached my car. I was about to speak when Hayden's lips found their way to mine. The unexpected yet deeply stirring kiss left me momentarily dazed, my mind racing. Hayden quickly apologized, "I'm sorry, I shouldn't have..." he began, but I was already reaching for him, drawn by an impulse I couldn't ignore.

Our second kiss was charged with an electric pulse, a mutual longing finally acknowledged. Surprised by my response, Hayden pulled away slightly, his breath ragged. "We shouldn't do this," he whispered, a conflict evident in his eyes.

At that moment, I knew what I wanted. "I want you," I confessed, my voice steady despite the whirlwind of emotions. "And I think you want me too. We could say goodbye and walk away right now if I am wrong."

Our eyes locked, and a silent conversation passed between us. As I reached to open my car door, Hayden's hand gently but firmly pushed it closed. "I want you," he confessed, his voice thick with emotion. "I've always wanted you, never stopped."

Our next kiss was a feverish mix of aching and anticipation. A dance of lips and breath that spoke volumes more than any words could. It was a connection, a passion I had never felt with Jackson. Hayden's lips were soft yet insistent, each touch sending waves of warmth through me, awakening a deep yearning for something more profound, something I had been missing for far too long.

As we finally parted, the unspoken agreement hung in the air – our night was barely getting started.

Chapter Twenty-Four

The moments following that intense second kiss with Hayden seemed to meld into a euphoric haze. I vaguely recall being swept into his truck, but the details of the journey to his apartment are a blur. It's the pulsing thrill of anticipation that I vividly remember as we arrived, his hand warmly enclosing mine; I followed the white rabbit down the rabbit hole, and boy, was it a good fall down that hole.

Once inside, the door shut and locked behind us; Hayden's actions were swift yet tender. In one fluid motion, he lifted me effortlessly, my legs instinctively wrapping around his waist. Our kiss deepened, a mingling of lustfulness and reckless abandon, as he carried me to the sanctuary of his bedroom.

There, he gently set me down, and his shirt was the first to go, discarded with an ease that matched his confident demeanor. His shoes were next, flung across the room in a moment of playful disregard that drew laughter from us both. Pants and underwear swiftly followed, revealing his striking form.

Standing before me, Hayden was the embodiment of rugged allure. His broad and inviting chest was adorned with a light dusting of chest hair, enhancing the muscular landscape beneath. His arms, toned and firm, harmonized with the defined contours of his abdomen. This vision of masculine grace was overpowering in its appeal. He looked so much better than I remember.

With a casualness that only heightened the moment's intensity, he removed my heels, jeans, and panties, each article of clothing joining the forgotten pile on the floor. My own shirt and bra soon joined them as we surrendered to the urgency of our desire.

Foreplay, at this moment, seemed an unnecessary delay. Our need was primal, immediate. As Hayden positioned himself above me and penetrated my tight moist slit, it was an exquisite fusion of pleasure and sweet pain — a stark reminder of the intimacy I'd been missing. Each of his thrusts ignited a spark within me, rekindling a fire that had long lain dormant. His lips claimed mine with each movement. Every taste of my essence found him drawn irresistibly deeper into the moment we shared.

Our hands found each other, fingers interlocking, stretching out above me. My legs wrapped around him, seeking to draw him deeper, to feel every inch of him. Lost in the rhythm of our connection, I barely noticed as his hand wandered, finding the epicenter of my pleasure.

His touch on my clitoris was both unfamiliar and electrifying, sending waves of euphoric chills cascading through me. The synchronization of his movements – his fingers circling my sensitive bud in rhythm with his deep, penetrating thrusts – quickened my breath and hastened my ascent to climax.

The world seemed to narrow to the sound of our shared breath and the feeling of him inside me. "God, Hayden," I gasped as an intense wave of pleasure crashed over me, the likes of which I'd never felt before. My nails instinctively clung to his back, marking him as mine, if only for this stolen moment. The overwhelming sensation spread through me, leaving me weak and deeply fulfilled.

With a teasing glint in her eye, Samantha couldn't help but giggle. "Bitch, was that your first real orgasm?"

I blushed slightly, admitting, "Yes, it was."

"Your ex did you dirty," she commented, shaking her head. "Whoever this Hayden is, he's got my stamp of approval."

I couldn't help but grin. "He's got mine too."

"Okay, go on," Samantha said, grabbing another chip.

"What else can I say?! That night was nothing short of spectacular," I started, reminiscing about the passionate encounter. "Hayden and I explored each other with an enthusiasm that I hadn't known I was missing. The experience was a revelation, taking me to heights of pleasure I hadn't thought possible, one earth-shattering orgasm after another."

Samantha's eyes widened in anticipation. "You can't just stop there," she urged. "I need all the dirty details!"

I hesitated, but her zeal was contagious. "Okay, okay. There was a moment that I can't help but replay in my mind when Hayden positioned himself above me. He teasingly rested his cock on my lips. I responded eagerly by opening my mouth and licking the tip. I watched in delight as he moaned at the warmth of my tongue on his member. He leaned forward and pushed his length into my mouth as far as it could go. He fucked my mouth savagely and relentlessly. The intensity in his eyes was mesmerizing.

Without warning, he turned the tables and started to flick my clit with the tip of his tongue. I moaned and began to squirm as he skillfully sucked my clit and fingered me all at once. I sucked his dick to match the rhythm of his fingers moving inside of me. He instinctively began to thrust deeper into my mouth as I moved my hips to meet each thrust of his fingers. His tongue is a thing of magic because that had to be the best orgasm of the night. I'll never forget how good he tasted as he came deep into my throat.

Samantha's energy was infectious. "YASSS Girl, YASSS!" she exclaimed, her excitement unmistakable. "That's what I am talking about! Those details are gold! Now, you've got to show me a picture of this Hayden."

I hesitated for a moment before diving into my phone's photo album. "Let's see if I have one," I said, though I knew well where to find his image. Scrolling through, I quickly found a photo Hayden had sent me a while back - him in his dress blues, looking every bit like the man who had ignited such passion in me. Handing my phone to Samantha, I watched her reaction.

She examined the photo, her eyes lighting up. "Uh-huh," she nodded, visibly impressed. " I can see why that's a face you like to sit on," she said with a cheeky grin, handing back my phone.

Her curiosity didn't wane. "So, I have to ask the inevitable: did you get caught?" she inquired.

I let out a sigh, the gravity of what had happened settling back in. "I lost all sense of time. When I woke up, the reality of the morning light hit me hard. It was almost 8:30 AM.

Panic set in as I saw Hayden still sleeping peacefully beside me. The weight of our actions began to dawn on me - the guilt, the exhilaration, the fear of the consequences. As I grappled with these thoughts, Hayden's phone suddenly broke the silence. To my utter shock, Jackson's name flashed on the screen. In that moment, time stood still, and I was frozen, caught between the aftermath of a passionate night and the impending reality of facing my husband."

The tension in the room skyrocketed as I urgently nudged Hayden awake, tossing his ringing phone at him. His confusion was evident as he groggily answered, hitting the green icon without a second thought.

"Hello?" Hayden's voice was thick with sleep.

The reply came clear and distinct, sending a chill down my spine. "Hey man, it's Jackson," said my husband, his voice unaware of the storm brewing on the other end.

Hayden's realization was instant; he shot upright, a mix of panic and recognition flashing in his eyes.

Jackson's voice continued, casual and unwitting. "Sorry I missed dinner last night; work was hell. I just didn't have it in me."

I seethed internally, labeling him a liar in my mind.

Trying to mask his sudden alertness, Hayden responded, "No worries, Jackson. I just wanted to catch up before I head out next week. I'm back in the Navy."

"Really? Good for you, man. I'm sure Kimber will fill me in on everything. She didn't come home last night, probably still mad about me bailing on dinner. You know, pregnancy hormones and all. She's likely cooling off at Marie's," Jackson speculated, his tone unconcerned.

Hayden, his frustration discernible, retorted, "You should give her a call, man. She's your pregnant wife. What if something happened?"

Jackson brushed it off, "I'm heading into work now. I don't want to start a thing over the phone. I'll sort it out when I get home. Keep in touch, and maybe we can hang out whenever you're on leave."

"Sure, take care," Hayden ended the call, a heavy silence enveloping us.

I lay back, feeling a mix of anger and astonishment. Jackson hadn't shown an ounce of concern for my absence. He was indifferent to the possibility of me being in any sort of trouble - all he cared about was work.

Sensing the turmoil churning inside me, Hayden gently pulled me into his embrace. Words were unnecessary; we just lay there, finding solace in each other's presence as the morning light bathed the room, highlighting the complexity of emotions that entangled us.

Samantha's shock was unmistakable as she processed my revelation. "So, you're telling me you were gone the entire night with another man, and Jackson didn't even flinch? No frantic calls or worried texts?"

I shrugged, a hint of bitterness lacing my voice. "Nothing. Not a fucking care to be had. I could've been stranded somewhere, in trouble. But no, his work was all that mattered."

"That's some bullshit!" Samantha exclaimed, her voice a mix of surprise and anger. "What did you do about it?"

"Nothing," I said calmly, sipping my margarita.

Samantha's mouth gaped open. "I'm sorry; what do you mean you did nothing?"

"Oh, you misunderstand. I did nothing at all with Jackson. I needed to bide my time and figure out a plan. But let's just say I continued to blissfully fuck Hayden sideways for the next five days. I meant what I said at dinner: we needed to make the most of his last days of freedom because, in all reality, they were the last days of mine as well. With Hayden, I felt liberated, alive in a way I hadn't since before Jackson came into my life. I knew the vibrant flame he rekindled in me would dim again once he left."

Samantha nodded in understanding, her eyes reflecting a blend of support and curiosity. "And after Hayden left? What happened then?"

Before I could delve further into the aftermath, my phone vibrated with an 'Unknown' caller ID.

"Excuse me a second," I said, standing up. "Hey, stranger," I answered, about to step away from the table.

Samantha's eyes widened in realization. "That's Hayden, isn't it?" She couldn't hide her excitement, her voice tinged with fascination.

I smiled mysteriously, my response teasing yet elusive. "Just as you said, that, my friend, is a tale for another happy hour," I replied, leaving Samantha with a sense of eager anticipation for the next chapter of my story.

Toxic Love

Paige

Chapter Twenty-Five

You know that feeling when you're just so fed up with guys that you can't even think straight? Well, that's me right now. I had all but given up on men, between being trapped in a cheating man's closet to another man making me sleep on the floor because I advised my friend not to sleep with his friend. It all played a part and it felt like it was too much. I owed it to myself to try something different. When I met Josh, things finally seemed to be heading in the right direction for me.

It was a spring, I was seated at a corner table of a local café, a solitary figure among the laid-back ambiance. I sat, tea in hand, enjoying the sanctuary of calm the café provided amidst the bustling world outside. As I savored the moment alone, memories of my romantic misadventures replayed like a bad movie in my mind. My most recent escapade involved being trapped in a closet and making a mad dash out of some lying-ass cheater's apartment. I couldn't help but chuckle at my predicament as I sipped my tea.

Yet, today marked a new beginning for me, a vow to venture beyond familiar disasters in search of something, someone, fundamentally different. Lost in contemplation, a shadow fell across my table. Lifting my gaze, I found myself entranced by the figure before me. A tall, handsome man stood there, his military uniform worn with undeniable pride. His chiseled features and piercing brown eyes exuded strength and confidence, yet a subtle hint of sadness lingered in their depths. I was inexplicably drawn to him as I watched him smile and take the seat across from me, an unspoken connection hanging in the atmosphere.

"Hi, I'm Josh," he said, extending his hand. His presence, so unexpected yet so right, left me momentarily speechless. "This is the part where you say nice to meet you, Josh, I am...," he said jokingly.

"Oh sorry, I'm Paige. Nice to meet you, Josh," I replied, feeling a blush coloring my cheeks.

Our conversation unfolded effortlessly, and hours slipped by as we delved into each other's worlds. Josh's charm and wit defied every preconception I had about soldiers. In his company, I found a connection so pure and intoxicating that it felt as if we had summoned each other into existence.

Six months later, moving in together felt like the inevitable next step, a crescendo in our symphony of shared dreams and laughter. Josh, a Marine of strength and tenderness, seemed to embody everything I yearned for. Yet, beneath his charming veneer, shadows lurked, unnoticed.

The initial weeks of cohabitation were like a dream, our love a fortress against the mundane challenges of shared life. His humor and affection made my heart race in the best way. But soon, the veil began to lift, revealing a pendulum that swung violently between adoration and abuse. His words, once sweet, now cut through me, leaving confusion and fear in their wake. Our discussions transformed into weekly battlegrounds, a war of words and emotions.

One Saturday afternoon, I sat on the couch, my expression a mix of anticipation and trepidation. Josh, on the other hand, leaned against the wall, his demeanor shifting between moments of charm and an unsettling edge. We were engaged in one of our weekly arguments.

"Remember those first few weeks, Josh? It was like living in a dream," I said, trying to smile.

"Yeah, it was something special," he agreed, nodding.

"We navigated through challenges and laughed at the little things. You were alluring, funny – the man who made my heart dance," I continued, leaning forward.

"I aim to please," he smirked.

"But then, something changed. You started swinging between being loving and being hurtful," I hesitated.

"What are you talking about?" he raised an eyebrow.

"One moment, you compliment me, making me feel cherished. Then the next, you insult my intelligence, and question my worth," I sighed.

"You're overreacting," he shrugged.

"Am I, Josh? It's like tiptoeing through an emotional minefield with you, one wrong step, and I'm left confused and hurt." My voice trembled.

"Look, I have my moods. Everyone does," he leaned in.

"It's more than moods, Josh. Our love is... chaotic. I'm trying to understand, but I feel like I'm losing myself in the process," I said, frustrated.

"I never asked you to lose yourself," he became defensive.

"No, but it's happening. I can't pretend everything's okay," I stood up, teary-eyed.

"You're making a big deal out of nothing," he smirked again.

"Is it nothing when you make my heart race for all the wrong reasons?" I challenged.

"Paige, I..."

"No, Josh. I need clarity, not more confusion," I interrupted, seeking a resolution he seemed unable to provide.

As our argument escalated, he stormed away, leaving me in shock. Refusing to let it end there, I followed him, calling out, "Wait, Josh, come back! Please don't leave."

In response, he turned and struck me, the impact sending me to the floor in disbelief.

"Why did you do that? Why?" I whispered, looking up at him with fear and shock.

Josh stood silent, his expression blank, retreating into himself—the man I loved, now a stranger. I struggled to comprehend this cruel transformation, my heart aching with a mix of fear and disbelief. I was left alone as he left the room, grappling with the reality of a love that had turned into a labyrinth of pain and confusion.

***

Two Years Later...

Two years had unfolded a complex narrative of emotions in our lives. Our journey together had been tumultuous, marked more by valleys than peaks. Amidst this chaotic dance, we had welcomed a beacon of hope, our son Cayden, six months prior. His arrival had cast a fleeting spell of tranquility over the perpetual storm that defined our relationship. However, like the deceptive calm before a storm, this period of peace was but a temporary relief. The storm lurking on the horizon was poised to unleash its fury once more, threatening to shatter the fragile serenity I had come to cherish.

"Josh, please. Can you stop yelling? I want you to calm down. I'm trying to help you," I implored, my voice a mix of desperation and concern.

"Help me? I don't need your help, okay? I'm perfectly fine. Mind your own business," Josh retorted, his voice laced with barely contained fury.

"But you're screaming at me. I'm just trying to do what's best for everyone. Let's talk, okay?" My voice trembled, seeking to defuse the situation.

"I don't need to talk to you. You're the one pushing me! Let me be, alright?" Josh's face was a mask of anger, his words like daggers.

"Josh, you have to listen to me. You need help. This behavior is not okay, especially not in front of our son," I pleaded, my voice cracking with emotion.

"What are you talking about? He's a baby! Let him grow up before making these assumptions," Josh snapped back, dismissive and defensive.

"Josh... I only want to help you. Please, give therapy a try," I begged, my eyes brimming with tears.

"What do you think a therapist is going to do? How will they fix me? It's all talk," Josh scoffed, his tone mocking.

"Josh, you have been diagnosed with PTSD. This isn't something you can fix on your own. Can't you see how much you've changed?" My voice was a whisper of despair.

"You think I want to be this way? It's exhausting, and I'm tired of it too. But I'm tired of being told what to do," Josh's voice broke, revealing a glimpse of the pain underneath his anger.

Our conversation took a dark turn as Josh's anger boiled over. He grabbed me, pinning me to the wall, our son Cayden in my arms. My voice was calm yet desperate, "Josh baby, let me go. Please, look at Cayden; you're scaring him."

Josh shook his head, his anger overwhelming his reason. "Just relax," he said flatly, his fingers digging into my arms as I struggled to hold Cayden.

"Josh, okay baby, I will let it go. Just let me go, please," I whispered, my voice trembling with fear.

"You're just saying that because you're scared. But you need to be punished. You need to know your place, Paige," Josh hissed through gritted teeth.

"Please, Josh. Don't do this," I pleaded, tears streaming down my face.

"Don't make me do this, Paige," Josh warned, his expression unchanged.

My heart raced with terror. "Don't do what, Josh?" I asked, my voice barely a whisper.

But Josh's attention shifted to Cayden, his hand raising towards the crying child. My protective instincts kicked in. "Josh! Don't you dare hurt my baby," I cried out.

Ignoring my pleas, Josh reached for Cayden's arm, bending it slowly, his face expressionless. Filled with horror, I screamed, "Josh, no!"

In sheer desperation, I shoved Josh with all my might, sending him and Cayden crashing against the wall. Seizing the opportunity, I kicked him, grabbed Cayden, and ran out of the apartment, screaming for help, my heart pounding with fear and adrenaline.

The night air echoed with my cries, a chilling reminder of the terrifying ordeal we had just endured.

How I Met Your Father

Kimber

Chapter Twenty-Six

"What the fuck was that?!" I asked as we sped away from the apartment complex, trying to process the evening's chaos.

Marie, equally flustered, threw her hands up in exasperation. "Exactly! Where did he vanish to all of a sudden?" Her voice was tinged with both confusion and frustration.

Christian, seemingly unfazed by the turmoil, reclined his seat slightly, finding comfort amidst the turmoil. "You know, it really could have been a lot worse," he commented, trying to find a silver lining.

Marie and I turned to him, incredulous. "Seriously, Christian?" we both exclaimed in unison, unable to believe his nonchalant attitude.

Pointing an accusing finger at him, I couldn't hold back. "This is on you! If you hadn't decided to end things with that lunatic, we wouldn't be in this mess," I argued, frustration clear in my voice.

Christian just flashed a mischievous grin. "But is it really, though?" His tone suggested he was almost enjoying the chaos.

As I navigated the truck back towards our neighborhood, my mind replayed the night's events. What was supposed to be a simple birthday dinner had somehow spiraled into an epic comedy of errors. And the root cause, you may ask? One word: **MASON!**

***

Earlier that afternoon...

"Seriously, how did my quiet birthday dinner turn into me tagging along on two of your dates?" Marie asked, her tone a mix of amusement and irritation.

"First off," I began, setting the record straight, "I'm not on a date with Christian. And secondly, I've been trying to dodge Mason for weeks. He's just not getting the hint. Since we work together, I thought it would be less awkward with you guys there, just in case."

"Uh huh," Marie responded, clearly not convinced. "You should have tried harder. I'm about to hang up on you."

"I did try!" I protested. "I told Mason tonight was about celebrating your birthday and spending time with Christian before he leaves again. But he wouldn't take no for an answer!"

"I find it real funny that my birthday was the chosen day for this," Marie teased.

"And I'm saying you're going to enjoy this evening, whether you like it or not. Remember your own Mason debacle last year that I had to endure?"

"Let's not revisit that," Marie quickly interjected.

I sang playfully, "Now I'm trapped in the closet toooo."

"Why bring that up?" Marie laughed, despite herself. "We agreed that was staying buried forever."

"You forced my hand," I retorted, still chuckling.

"Fine," Marie conceded. "I'll put on a happy face for tonight and probably be a little high. That's the only way I am getting through this. Quick question though, when will you admit there's something going on between you and Christian?"

"I don't know what you're talking about," I replied, feigning ignorance.

Marie wasn't having it. "Don't play dumb with me. You two obviously have feelings for each other. He's the only man you really talk to, and you always light up around him. I haven't seen you this way with anyone else, not even your ex-husband."

"It's not like that," I insisted. "Christian is just like a male version of you."

"I'm not buying it," Marie said, ending the call with a knowing tone. "That's your person! See you at six."

I hung up, left contemplating the idea of Christian and me. My history with men had been chaotic, culminating in a loveless marriage and a string of military boyfriends. I sometimes felt I had a stamp on my forehead that read, "Military apply here."

Christian was different, though. When Christian first entered my life, he was far removed from the world of the military, instead immersed in the realm of healthcare, much like myself—a refreshing and familiar parallel. But as our paths intertwined over two years, he, too, made the unexpected shift into military life. It's undeniable that our conversations became the soundtrack of my days; we talked incessantly, finding solace in each other's words whenever our work didn't consume us. He evolved into the sole man whose presence I yearned for, the only voice I eagerly anticipated.

Yet, for reasons I couldn't quite fathom, I hesitated to cross that unspoken boundary. Did my heart harbor deeper feelings for him? What path was I forging in this complex web of emotions? As I felt my mental troops rallying for another round of deep introspection, a glance at the clock showing 2:15 PM prompted me to opt for a nap instead until it was time to prepare for the evening's plans.

At 5:45 PM, I arrived at Marie's, only to be playfully chided for being early. We soon set off, our ride filled with silence until I missed the exit for the restaurant. Marie's confusion was evident.

"Where are you going? You missed the exit," Marie asked, confused.

"We need to pick Mason up," I sighed.

"I know you are fucking lying," Marie begins. "Not only did he crash my birthday, he has no car?!"

"Fun facts I found out today when I messaged the restaurant address," I admitted.

Marie, meticulously adjusting her lipstick, offered a sardonic conclusion. "Well, in that case, he would have just been sitting at home, wouldn't he?" Her tone mixes humor with a dash of scorn.

Her mood only soured further as we navigated through Mason's less-than-desirable neighborhood.

"This is the hood," she remarked, surveying our surroundings.

"Yep," I agreed, texting Mason our arrival. A knock on the window startled us as we contemplated leaving the sketchy apartment complex.

"Hey, did I scare you?" Mason greeted us cheerily, unaware of the tension he had just walked into.

As I unlocked the car door, Mason, to my surprise, opened the front passenger door instead of heading to the back. He stood there expectantly, waiting for Marie to relocate to the back seat. Marie's face was a picture of barely restrained irritation. I bit my lip to stop myself from laughing at the absurdity of the situation.

I made the introductions as smoothly as I could under the circumstances. "Mason, this is Marie. Marie, meet Mason," I said, trying to ease the tension.

Marie, visibly annoyed, hastily exited the passenger side and clambered into the back seat, throwing Mason a look that could melt steel. "I see," she muttered, her tone frosty.

Once Mason settled comfortably into the passenger seat, his grin spread wide with an air of blissful ignorance. "I'm really looking forward to tonight," he announced with an upbeat tone, reaching out to take my hand. His cheerful demeanor starkly contrasted with the growing hostility within the car, rendering the atmosphere even more uncomfortable.

Reacting instinctively, I gently withdrew my hand and offered a non-committal "Uh huh," focusing on steering the truck out of the neighborhood and onto the freeway. In the rearview mirror, Marie's expression was a mix of amusement and 'That's-what-you-get,' clearly enjoying the predicament I had found myself in.

Only five minutes into what felt like a never-ending twenty-minute drive, Mason's ceaseless chatter had already frayed my nerves. He rambled on without a pause for air, oblivious to my rising aggravation. Desperate for a distraction, I reached for the stereo and cranked up the volume on the loudest Slipknot track I could find. The heavy metal riffs blasted through the speakers as I rolled down the windows, the wind whipping through the truck.

In the backseat, Marie was in fits of laughter, thoroughly entertained by the unfolding scene. Meanwhile, I pushed the truck to 80 mph, as I had never wanted to escape the confines of my truck so badly then at that moment.

Chapter Twenty-Seven

Arriving at Atchafalaya Eats, a Louisiana-inspired gem, the parking ordeal was a test of patience. The new mall extension, a magnet for crowds, had turned the area into a maze of cars and bustling shoppers. Finally snagging a spot, I quickly messaged Christian to inform him of our arrival. He was still weaving his way through traffic, about five minutes out.

The restaurant greeted us with the soulful rhythms of zydeco music. The ambiance was a delightful mix of New Orleans's best and Mardi Gras. Mason's eyes lit up in awe as we approached the hostess.

"This place is incredible," he remarked, clearly captivated.

"A table for four, please," I requested at the hostess booth.

The hostess informed us of a brief wait, handing me a pager to signal when our table was ready. With some time to spare, we ventured across the courtyard to the Candy Factory, a sweet escape from Mason's endless aviation maintenance tales and giving Christian enough time to catch up.

Just as the colorful confections of the Candy Factory came into view, my phone rang – it was Christian. "Thank you, Lord," I thought to myself. He was already at the mall but seemed lost and unfamiliar with the new extension.

"Hey guys, I have to run and get Christian. He's lost in the mall," I announced, making a beeline for the exit.

"We'll come with you," Marie insisted, shooting me a knowing look.

"Not necessary," I replied with a smile, escaping before they could join.

As I walked past the Candy Factory, Marie's glare through the window was unmistakable, especially as Mason casually put his arm around her and waved.

The thought crossed my mind, bringing an internal chuckle. "She's going to kill me," I mused to myself.

Navigating through the sea of people inside the mall, I contacted Christian.

"Where are you?" I inquired.

"Near Dillard's," he replied.

Scanning the area, I replied, "I don't see you, and I'm right in front of Dillard's."

"I see you, though," he said, tapping me on the shoulder.

"Shit, you scared me," as I turned laughing, ending the call and embracing him. I found Christian, somehow taller and more muscular than my memory served. His simple attire of jeans and shirt did nothing to hide his newfound physique. Our hug lingered, his cologne enveloping me in a blend of sweet and spicy notes, stirring unfamiliar feelings and making it hard to let go.

As we broke away, I realized my usual ease with him had been replaced by a flurry of nerves.

"We should head back to Marie before she kills Mason," I joked, trying to regain composure.

As we walked, Christian asked, "Yeah, how's that date going?"

"It's something," I replied, filling him in on the evening's events, and his laughter echoed through the mall.

"This is going to be priceless," he said, mischief in his eyes.

"Please don't do anything," I pleaded, knowing his penchant for pranks.

He circled a halo above his head, pretending innocence.

I led the way to the Candy Factory. Peering inside, we saw no sign of Marie and Mason. Confused, we eventually found them outside the restaurant. Christian paused, "What the hell is that in her hand?"

Marie stood there, clutching a cat plushie, her smile tight and eyes twitching with unconcealed irritation.

As we approached Marie and Mason, curiosity piqued, I inquired, "Whatcha got there?"

Holding a stuffed toy, Marie explained, "It's some cat. He bought it at the Candy Factory as a birthday gift. I told him it wasn't necessary, but he insisted."

Mason chimed in with a hint of pride, "It's Pusheen," expecting a flicker of recognition from us.

We exchanged puzzled glances, our collective ignorance noticeable.

"It's a cartoon cat," Mason elaborated, hoping to enlighten us.

"Not ringing any bells," Christian admitted, breaking the awkward silence.

Undeterred, Mason extended a similar plushie to me. "I got you one too."

Surprised, I responded, "Oh, that's really thoughtful, but you didn't have to."

"But I wanted to," Mason insisted, moving in for a hug. "This is going to be great, you and me. I can feel it," he declared, embracing me a bit too snugly.

In a silent plea for rescue, I glanced at Christian, who met my gaze with a puzzled expression.

"Looks like our table might be ready," Christian interjected, smoothly guiding me away from Mason's embrace and towards the restaurant.

Arriving at the hostess booth, I realized with relief that our table was indeed ready. Christian excused himself to the restroom as the hostess showed us to our table. As we reached our booth, Marie and I began a subtle game of musical chairs, neither eager to sit next to Mason. Eventually, Mason and Marie took opposite sides of the booth, with Mason invitingly patting the seat beside him. Suppressing her laughter, Marie teased, "Yes, best friend, take a seat."

Resigned, I sank into the seat next to Mason, feeling him inch closer.

Tyler, our waiter, arrived to take our drink orders. His brisk tone and terse demeanor hinted at a challenging day, adding another layer of complexity to an already eventful evening.

"Hey, I'm Tyler, your waiter for the evening. Is this your first time here?" Tyler asked with a lack of enthusiasm that was hard to miss.

Marie and I simultaneously responded, "No," while Mason chimed in with a "Yes."

Tyler's response was a lackluster "Great. What can I get you to drink?"

We all opted for water, and Tyler left to fetch them, his lack of enthusiasm trailing behind him.

Christian returned to the table as we browsed the menu, his arrival punctuating the uncomfortable silence.

Tyler soon returned with our waters. "Oh, I didn't realize you had a fourth person," he remarked, placing the glasses on the table.

"Yes indeed," Christian said with a smile. "And you are?"

"Tyler," I interjected a hint of dryness in my voice, recalling his earlier introduction.

"Good evening, Tyler. This is my first visit. What would you recommend?" Christian inquired, his tone polite and engaging.

This seemed to pique Tyler's interest as he enthusiastically began detailing his favorite drinks and dishes. Marie and I exchanged a glance, both of us wondering where this newfound warmth had been when we first sat down. I couldn't help but feel a bit amused as Christian and Tyler bantered about the menu options.

After taking Christian's order, Tyler turned to the rest of us with a markedly less eagerness, "Do you know what you want?"

Internally, I couldn't help but think, "What the hell?"

Marie and I ordered seafood fondeaux and a dozen chargrilled oysters to share. Christian ordered the Redfish Pontchartrain. Mason, however, opted for a hamburger – a rather unconventional choice in a seafood-centric establishment.

"You're just getting a hamburger?" Marie asked, her tone laced with surprise.

"Yes," Mason replied confidently, "The description in the menu made it sound delicious."

Marie shrugged as we handed our menus back to Tyler.

"I'll be back with your drink," Tyler said to Christian, seemingly oblivious to the rest of us.

I couldn't resist a playful jab, "Do we need to give you and Tyler some alone time?"

Christian chuckled in response, "No, no, we're good."

"He's treating us like we're an afterthought while he seems quite taken with you," I pointed out to Christian.

Marie nodded in agreement. "Yeah, I did notice that," Christian conceded with a hint of acknowledgment.

Just then, Mason edged closer to me, coolly draping his arm around my shoulder. I couldn't help but stiffen at the gesture. Noticing my discomfort, Christian swiftly diverted the conversation. "So, Mason, what do you do for a living?"

Mason perked up. "Well, I'm currently working valet at a hospital, but my passion is aviation maintenance. I'm still finishing school, but flying planes is my dream. The valet job is a stepping stone to buy a car."

As Mason delved into his aspirations, Marie and I subtly tuned out, having already endured this narrative earlier. Another round of aviation maintenance talk was more than we could handle.

"Really?" Christian engaged, "What kind of car are you interested in?"

"A truck would be ideal. Actually, a truck like Kimber's would be perfect," Mason replied with a hint of longing.

Christian played along, "You're in luck; I know someone with a truck just like that."

Mason's face brightened at the prospect. Seizing the moment, I discreetly nudged Christian under the table, a silent plea to stop teasing.

"Ow," Christian exclaimed, drawing a curious glance from Mason.

"About that truck..." Mason started.

Christian, catching my stern look, quickly backpedaled. "Actually, disregard what I said," he corrected, defusing the situation.

My patience was thin as Tyler briskly arrived with Christian's drink and our much-anticipated food.

"That was quick," I remarked with a hint of relief at the sight of our meal.

Tyler, however, seemed oblivious to my comment. He quickly placed the dishes on the table and turned to Christian, "Do you need anything else?"

Christian replied, "No, I'm good, thanks.

Tyler left with a fleeting smile, completely ignoring the rest of us. I couldn't help but throw my hands up and say, "What are we...chopped liver?"

Christian, noticing my lack of amusement, couldn't help but laugh. I rolled my eyes and turned towards Mason, only to find that he had already polished off his entire hamburger. Astonished, I could barely utter a word as he said, "That was amazing. You know what would be even better?" We all looked as if to say, "What?" Without skipping a beat, Mason eagerly proposed, "We should all share food," reaching with his fork to scoop a generous portion of Marie's fondeaux.

Christian and I quickly shielded our plates from potential invasion. Appalled yet sarcastic, Marie remarked, "Well, help yourself."

In a swift move, Mason commandeered Marie's entire plate. I struggled to stifle my laughter while Christian scanned the room for Tyler, realizing our dinner was spiraling out of control.

"Christian, let me out," Marie demanded, sliding out of the booth and heading straight for the door.

When Tyler returned, Christian requested two to-go boxes and the checks. "How do you want the checks split?" Tyler inquired.

Christian, gesturing to himself and Marie, said, "I'll cover myself and the birthday girl here."

"That's so sweet," I commented, genuinely touched by his gesture. Christian joked, "It's the least I can do after Fondeaux Gate," pointing to me and Mason for a separate check.

Mason interjected, "I can only cover my meal. You'll need to pay for your own."

This declaration drew unbelieving looks from all of us. "Yeah, I spent $50 on those Pusheen cats," Mason says indifferently.

"You did what?" Christian exclaimed in disbelief.

I offered Mason the plushie back, "We can return these right now."

Brushing his hand against my face, Mason insisted, "No, it's a symbol of our growing love."

Christian sighed heavily, turning back to Tyler, "Put me down for myself and the two ladies, and he'll cover himself."

Tyler nodded, barely concealing his amusement.

Annoyed, I excused myself, "I'm going to check on Marie."

Outside, I found her sitting on a bench. Sitting beside her, I said, "Girl, I don't even know where to start. If he touches me one more time, he might lose his damn hand."

Marie chuckled, "I can't believe he just devoured his meal and then proceeded to Hoover Vac mine."

"Right? Who suggests sharing after they've finished their own meal?" I questioned, equally baffled.

"The fucker's gots to go. GO," Marie declared. "

I bust out laughing. "Who are you telling?!" I said, in agreeance.

Just then, Christian and Mason emerged. "Where to next?" Mason asked, visibly excited.

"Home," Marie stated firmly.

Mason, undeterred, suggested, "Or, we could hit a liquor store, grab a bottle, and chill in the bed of your truck."

We exchanged glances before unanimously responding, "No," as we began walking towards the parking lot.

Chapter Twenty-Eight

Arriving at my truck, I unlocked the doors and climbed into the driver's seat while Marie settled in the back. A silent, awkward standoff unfolded between Mason and Christian on the passenger side. With a look of quiet assertion, Christian seemed to communicate that he wasn't budging from the front seat. I rested my head on the steering wheel momentarily, pondering the night's misadventures. The sound of the doors closing signaled the end of the standoff, and I felt Christian's comforting pat on my back, indicating he had secured the front seat.

Turning to Marie through the rearview mirror, I said, "Marie, this night didn't quite go as planned. How about we head to Whiskey Cowboy? We can dance, enjoy some free drinks, play a bit of pool, then call it a night."

Marie, appreciating my effort to salvage her birthday evening, smiled and agreed, "Sounds like fun, let's do it."

Mason started to interject with another absurd recommendation, but sensing another outrageous suggestion looming, I quickly started the truck and connected my phone, and Christian, sensing my intention, cranked up the volume. The thunderous tones of Slipknot filled the truck as we pulled out of the parking spot, heading to Whiskey Cowboy. Mason reclined, realizing his suggestion was overruled.

The fifteen-minute drive, accompanied by heavy metal, gave us a much-needed break to reset. Whiskey Cowboy was buzzing with activity, typical for a Saturday night. After finding a parking spot, Marie and I approached the entrance.

"One round of pool, two dances, two shots, and then we head home," Marie proposed, gripping my arm.

"I was thinking more like one, one, and one, but it's your birthday. Let's make the most of it!" I replied enthusiastically.

As we reached the entrance, I showed my ID to the bouncer, followed by Marie.

"Ladies, get in free," he announced, stamping our hands.

"Thank you," we responded in unison, stepping inside.

Christian presented his military ID next. "Military gets in free, and you get a free drink. Thank you for your service," the bouncer informed him, handing over a drink card and stamping his hand.

"Great, thanks," Christian responded, joining us inside.

We stood waiting for Mason as we heard "What is this?" from the bouncer. This prompted us to peek back outside. "I don't know what that is, but I need your ID," the bouncer said, annoyed, handing Mason back the mystery card. Mason awkwardly dug in his wallet finally producing his ID. The bouncer gives it a once over before saying, "It will be $10 at the cashier," motioning him to enter.

We breezed past the cashier, our stamps evident, when Mason called out, "I have to pay!" The cashier halted him, and he turned to us, sheepishly admitting, "Hey guys, I don't have the money." We paused, a silent huddle of contemplation until Christian generously handed him $10. "You're a better man," I say, leaning gratefully against Christian's arm. He smiled, realizing I would have left Mason at the door. "Come on, silly, let's toast to the birthday girl, shall we?"

At the bar, Christian efficiently caught the bartender's attention and ordered eight birthday cake shots. Trying to edge closer between Christian and me, Mason inadvertently inhaled Christian's cologne, leading him to an unexpected reaction. He turned Christian around and began to sniff him enthusiastically. Marie and I exchanged glances of shock and horror. "Whoa, what's happening here?!" Christian exclaimed, hands raised in surprise.

Mason, fixated on Christian's scent, remarked with a captivated tone, "You smell amazing. What's that fragrance?"

"Polo Red, I believe," Christian replied, visibly uncomfortable with the attention.

As the bartender placed our shots on the counter, her face mirrored the oddity of the situation. Eager to move past the awkward exchange, Christian thanked her and settled the bill.

Still locked onto Christian, Mason asked in a tone of naive surprise, "You have to pay for drinks here?"

Marie couldn't hide her sarcasm as she retorted, "Sir, it's pretty standard to pay for drinks at a bar."

Unfazed, Mason said, "Not at the places I hang out."

We all frowned at his response, though we were each slightly intrigued to know more.

"Not worth it," I say, reading their thoughts.

His comment piqued a curious silence among us, each one momentarily tempted to dive deeper into Mason's peculiar world.

Sensing their curiosity, I quickly intervened, "Trust me, it's not worth it." My tone hinted that some mysteries were better left unsolved.

"Right," Christian says as he distributes the shots. Marie leaned in, "Let's just do one round of each and call it a night."

We toasted to Marie. "Happy Birthday, bestie!" I said excitedly.

"Happy Birthday, Marie. Looking forward to many more with you," Mason added.

Marie, nearly choking on her shot at the thought of more birthdays with Mason, quickly diverted, "Look, an open pool table!" and swiftly exited towards it, shot still in hand.

As we set our glasses down, Mason excitedly announced, "Wait, free popcorn!" Ignoring my warning that "Nobody eats that," he was already filling his mouth and bags with popcorn.

Christian shook his head, "It's like watching a train wreck," as he headed towards the pool table. Slightly disgusted, I glanced at my phone; it read 9:40 PM. The night had been a rollercoaster, and my bed was calling me as I walked to the pool table.

Mason arrived at the pool table with a cue stick in hand and crunching popcorn. "I love the pool," he declared, oblivious to the chaos he'd stirred.

"Great, you can rack them then," I proclaimed.

As Mason took his turn to rack the balls, I suggested, "Let's go with teams. How about men versus women?" Christian, Marie, and I each picked up cue sticks, ready for the friendly challenge.

I watched Mason arrange the balls, then scowled. "I don't think you've got that right, Mason. But I'm no pool expert," Christian remarked, glancing at me for confirmation.

Mason defensively asserted, "Of course it's right. I play all the time."

With a sigh, I stepped in, "Actually, you've got it mixed up. The balls should alternate between solids and stripes, with the eight ball in the center, not at the front." I adjusted the arrangement accordingly.

Meanwhile, Marie, seeming detached from the unfolding drama, slumped onto a bar stool, resting her head on the table.

Once the balls were correctly racked, I asked Mason, "Can you break?" casting doubt on his proclaimed expertise.

His reply was brimming with overconfidence, "Of course I can." His break, however, resulted in no balls pocketed. I followed, smoothly sinking a solid in the corner pocket.

The game dragged on. With all the stools occupied, I casually sat on Christian's lap, causing him to whisper in surprise, "What are you doing?"

"Just sitting. No seats left," I responded coolly, noting how my proximity seemed to fluster him.

Observing our interaction, Marie coughed loudly, drawing attention to Mason's glaring disapproval.

As the game of pool lost its appeal, "The Wobble" came on, and I grabbed Marie for a dance.

Amidst our moves, Marie shouted over the music, "You and Christian were pretty cozy."

"And?" I replied, trying to be nonchalant.

Marie teased, "You two look good together. But I think someone's not too happy about it."

I grimaced at the thought of Mason. "We've hit all our targets for the night. Time to wrap up, I think." I start walking towards the dance floor exit leaving Marie trailing behind me.

Marie pressed on, "Just admit you like Christian. It's obvious he's into you," as she followed after me.

Before I could change the subject, a cowboy-clad gentleman approached me, asking me for a dance. As I hesitated, Marie jumped in, "She'd love to," nudging me towards him. I smiled, allowing him to lead me in a lively dance.

"Where's Kimber?" Mason pressed as Marie arrived back at the table.

"She's dancing with a cowboy," Marie informed him as she settled at our table. "I think we're done with pool."

Christian, visibly relieved, promptly put down his cue stick. "Thank God," he exclaimed, returning to his seat with a sense of finality.

A tense silence enveloped the table for a few minutes before Christian, turning to Mason, inquired, "So, how do you think your date's going?"

Marie, engrossed in her phone, barely noticed the question.

Unaware of the undercurrents, Mason replied with unsettling enthusiasm, "I think it's going great. I really like her. She's perfect for what I have in mind."

Marie, now drawn away from her phone, exchanged a puzzled glance with Christian.

Christian, probing further, asked, "What does that even mean?"

With chilling confidence, Mason elaborated, "Perfect to marry and take back to Oregon. I've got land there. I'm planning to build and live off-grid. Like I said, she will be perfect."

Unable to contain herself, Marie interjected, "You're not dragging my friend off on some wild Oregon trail fantasy!"

Mason's smile didn't waver. "She'll come willingly."

Christian stood up abruptly, his tone stern, "This date is over! Kimber doesn't like you; I don't like you, and you're deluded if you think you have a future with her. Back off and leave her alone."

Marie tried to intervene, "Christian, maybe we should—"

Mason, defiant, retorted, "You can't tell me what to do. Who the fuck do you think you are? I do believe she's on the date with me, not you."

Christian's voice was unwavering. "I've been in her life way before you showed up and I'll be here long after you're gone. I suggest you find someone else for your creepy Oregon shitshow, but leave Kimber out of it. She's mine," he stated firmly before walking away.

Marie, momentarily caught up in the drama, couldn't help but admire Christian's protectiveness. "Damn, that's hot," she murmured, watching him leave. "Wish my husband was like that."

Snapping back to reality, she realized she was alone at the table with a now-infuriated Mason.

"Shit," she said to herself.

Chapter Twenty-Nine

Exhausted from the dance, I declared, "I don't think I can manage another dance," as I made my way off the dance floor.

Travis, catching up, offered, "At least let me buy you a drink?"

"I really should get back to my friends," I insisted, descending the stairs.

"Just one quick drink," he urged with a charming smile.

I relented, "Okay," and followed him to the bar.

Travis smoothly got the bartender's attention and ordered two beers, engaging in casual conversation.

Suddenly, Christian appeared beside me. "We need to leave, now," he said urgently.

Puzzled, I asked, "Why? What happened?"

"I just broke up with James for you, and he's pissed. We have to go," he blurted out.

Stunned, I exclaimed, "You WHAT?!" as Christian tugged me towards the exit.

Apologizing to Travis, I hurried out with Christian.

Outside, I stormed towards my car, with Christian now trailing behind. "Are you mad?" he asked, struggling to keep pace.

Frustrated, I fumbled with my car keys. "Why on Earth would you do something like that, especially when we still have to ride back with him? It's not your place to decide who I date!"

Christian countered, "Because it needed to happen, and I saved you the trouble. Don't act like you were head over heels for that weirdo."

I shake my head, "That's not the point," as I open the truck door and climb in.

"Then why invite me tonight? I thought you wanted to see me before I left," Christian remarks climbing into the passenger seat.

I slammed the car door shut, "Yes, I did want to see you! I wanted tonight to be about us, not this mess."

He looked at me, surprised. "You did?"

"Yes," I confessed, meeting his gaze. "I enjoy being with you, Christian. I like you."

His expression softened, a mix of shock and vulnerability. "I thought we were just friends, especially after you turned me down before. I didn't realize you felt that way."

I hesitated, then admitted, "Two years ago, I knew I had feelings for you, but I pushed you away. You're the one I look forward to talking to every day. I've always had feelings for you, Christian. I was just too afraid to admit it."

Christian's gaze held mine with an intensity that felt like it could ignite the very air between us. "I've always had feelings for you, too, even when you pushed me away. I never stopped," he confessed.

His words resonated deeply, but I couldn't let go of what had transpired earlier. "It still doesn't make it okay that you broke up with Mason on my behalf," I began, ready to express my frustration. But before I could delve into a full tirade, Christian's lips met mine, silencing my protests with a kiss that was both unexpected and electrifying.

He pulled back slightly, a question in his eyes. "Is this okay?"

"Definitely," I replied, leaning in to kiss him again, our pent-up emotions unraveling with every touch.

As I maneuvered myself onto his lap, I insisted, "It still doesn't make it okay, though," even as I continued to kiss him, unable to resist the magnetic pull between us.

"He was about to drag you off to Oregon and turn you into a collectible sister wife," Christian half-joked between kisses.

I paused, pulling back in surprise. "Wait...WHAT???" I asked, bewildered by his revelation.

***

Marie, uncomfortably seated at the table, silently cussing Christian and me out in her mind, while Mason continued his furious rant.

"Who the fuck does he think he is?" Mason fumed. "She's missing out big time! I'm a damn good catch."

Marie, dumbfounded by his outburst, could only offer a noncommittal shrug and a blunt, "That's fucked up."

"Right?!" Mason agreed, seeming to find validation in her words. He then turned to Marie, who was frantically texting me in hopes of an escape. "You on Facebook?" he asked, a hopeful smile on his face.

"Uh, yeah," Marie replied, caught off guard.

"Add me," Mason insisted, showing her his profile, maintaining uncomfortable eye contact.

With little choice, Marie reluctantly added him on Facebook. But instead of ending the conversation, Mason began boasting, showing her photos of his paycheck stubs and properties. "Look at this," he said, "All from one week's work."

Marie responded with a feigned, unenthusiastic "Oh wow," her patience wearing thin. Finally, realizing there was no end in sight to this madness, Marie simply stood up and headed for the exit, hoping to leave the unpleasant situation behind.

As she made her way out, she realized Mason was following close behind. With a resigned sigh, she accepted the inevitable company. Upon reaching the truck, Marie was met with an unexpected sight – Christian and I, completely lost in a full-blown make out session in the front seat of my truck.

Marie's initial reaction to seeing Christian and me was a triumphant "Yes!" – thrilled that we finally acknowledged our long-hidden feelings. However, she quickly remembered that Mason was behind her, and she couldn't let him see us, which would make an already bad night worse.

Turning to Mason, she faked concern, "Oh shit, I think I left my phone back in the bar," patting her pockets for effect. "Could you run back and check for me?"

"Sure thing," Mason replied eagerly, turning back towards the bar.

Seizing the opportunity, Marie dashed to the truck, pounding on the passenger window to get our attention.

Startled from kissing, Christian and I looked up to find Marie glaring at us through the window.

"I can't believe we forgot about Marie," I said, guilt creeping in.

"Yeah, I guess I did kind of cause a scene and then just left," Christian admitted sheepishly.

Impatient with our slow reaction, Marie swung the passenger door open. "First off, I love this, and I'm thrilled for you two," she said with genuine warmth. But her tone quickly shifted, "However, you left me with that psycho. If we don't get moving, he is liable to turn all three of us into lampshades if he sees this shit!"

We quickly rearranged ourselves, Christian helping me climb out of the truck. Mason appeared as I moved around to the driver's side, glaring intensely at me. He walked past without breaking his stare, then got into the back seat, leaving an unsettling silence in his wake.

"This is going to be awkward," I thought climbing back into the truck.

The silence inside the vehicle was discernible as we left the Whiskey Cowboy parking lot. No one dared to break it, fearing it might stir up more trouble. The freeway entrance greeted us with a standstill traffic jam. Marie's murmured "Great" echoed the collective frustration in the car, especially given her eagerness to escape Mason in the backseat.

Christian and I exchanged glances, both yearning to return to our moment of solitude before the interruption. As we inched forward, the cause of the delay became apparent – a rolled vehicle was blocking two lanes.

"So, we're rubbernecking now," I muttered, my annoyance clear.

Marie chimed in, "I don't get why everyone has to slow down just to gawk."

Unexpectedly, Mason shouted, "People died! Show some respect!"

Puzzled, Christian asked, "Where?" as we could only see people arguing beside the accident site, presumably about who was at fault.

"They died," Mason repeated ominously.

The bizarre comment left us all speechless, unsure of how to react. It was clear Mason was already teetering on instability, so we sat rigidly, looking straight ahead, silently pleading for the car ride to end.

Once past the accident, I drove with a newfound urgency, eager to reach Christian's apartment. Pulling into the complex, I threw the truck into park and got out, intending to apologize for how the night had unfolded. But when I turned around, Mason had vanished without a trace.

"He's gone," I said, baffled.

Marie, equally perplexed, exclaimed, "What do you mean? He was just there!"

As we scanned the area, it was evident he hadn't entered any nearby apartments.

"He just vanished into the night?" Christian asked, still searching.

Marie urged, "Get your ass back in the car, let's go before the night gets any weirder."

I climbed back in, still in shock. "What the fuck just happened?" I asked as we sped away.

Marie, throwing her hands up, echoed my confusion, "Exactly! Where did he go?"

Christian, surprisingly calm, reclined his seat. "It could've been worse," he mused.

Marie and I shot him incredulous looks. "Seriously, Christian?" we both said in unison.

I pointedly accused him, "This is your fault! If you hadn't decided to end things with that lunatic, we wouldn't have been in this mess..."

Christian grinned cheekily. "But did I really make it worse? I got you, didn't I?" he said, taking my hand....

Six years later, in our nursery, Christian steps in, as he had been listening to the story the whole time. "I always knew you'd come around," he said, watching me rock our baby, Avery.

"Did you, though?" I smiled, looking down at our daughter. "I know, Avery. Daddy thinks he's a know-it-all. But that's the story of how I met your father."

"Well, kind of," Christian added playfully to Avery. "We'll have to wait until you are a little older for that one."

Afterword

We want to express our heartfelt gratitude to each and every
one of you who embarked on the journey of our first book with
us. It's been a long-awaited dream finally coming to fruition, and
your support has meant the world to us.

By now, you've likely discovered that there's more to the story.
Yes, you heard it right! We couldn't bear to leave you hanging,
and we're excited to announce the upcoming release of the
second installment in the series. The girls have plenty more tales
to share, and their cups runneth over with juicy stories.

If our stories resonated with you and brought a smile to your
face, we kindly invite you to show your support. It could be as
simple as clicking those shining stars on the retailer's website,
hitting the 'LIKE' button, or even taking a moment to pen a
review on Goodreads. Your feedback means the world to us, and
it helps us grow as storytellers. We can't wait to hear your
thoughts and share more adventures with you. So, stay tuned
for Tales From An Average Girl: The Messy Chronicles Part Two!

Kimber & Marie

9 798869 204752